THE TWO WIVES OF MILLARD FILLMORE

NFB
Buffalo, New York

The Two Wives of Millard Fillmore

Rachelle Moyer Francis

Copyright © 2024 By Rachelle Moyer Francis

Printed in the United States of America

The Two Wives of Millard Fillmore / Francis 1st Edition

ISBN: 978-1-953610-86-7

Nonfiction> History>United States
Nonfiction> History>Presidents
Nonfiction> History
Nonfiction>Biography

No part of this book may be reproduced or transmitted in any form by any means, electronic or mechanical, including photocopying, recording, or by any information storage and retrieval system without permission in writing by the author.

The map on page 12 and the cover art is by Bethany Brynn Francis.

NFB Publishing
119 Dorchester Road
Buffalo, New York 14213
For more information visit Nfbpublishing.com

To a meticulous editor,
a ready adventurer,
and the best of friends,
Karen Stuart Williams

CONTENTS

CHAPTER 1—ABIGAIL'S ROOTS	11
CHAPTER 2—MARRIAGE IN EAST AURORA	17
CHAPTER 3—WIDENING WORLD IN THE THIRTIES	23
CHAPTER 4—THE FORTIES	31
CHAPTER 5—A STINT IN ALBANY AND BACK TO DC	41
CHAPTER 6—POLITICAL PITFALLS OF 1850	47
CHAPTER 7— LIVING IN THE WHITE HOUSE	53
CHAPTER 8—SAD RETURN TO BUFFALO	65
CHAPTER 9— FORGETTING OUR TROUBLES	75
CHAPTER 10—CAROLINE'S ROOTS AND MARRIAGES	81
CHAPTER 11—CAROLINE'S TROUBLED WIDOWHOOD	95
CHAPTER 12—POSTSCRIPT	105

PREAMBLE

Both wives were blue bloods with roots to the Puritans. One never had children; the other was a devoted mother of two. One savored education above all; the other loved to shop. But both were chosen by the same man, the most impoverished man ever to become president of the United States.

AUTHOR'S NOTES:

This is a new sort of biography in that I used many authentic words from newspapers and letters from the actual time period. Perhaps it is a "fractured memoir." I chose to write the two women's stories in two voices—Abigail in her own voice, Caroline in her stepson's voice. Rather than distracting the reader with confusing quotation marks, the story is heavily footnoted. I hope readers find it enlightening in the changing roles of womanhood in the 19th century and that the same man can marry once for love and once for money.

The term "First Lady" was not used until referring to Frances Folsom Cleveland in 1886 and then more regularly in the 20th Century. I chose to use the term "first lady of the White House" instead to describe Abigail Fillmore's position.

I used the term "East Aurora" loosely. The two villages—Willink and East Aurora--during this time period went through several name changes. Again, I chose not to confuse the reader by not including all the name fluidity.

A new, and I believe, untapped source is the collection of scrapbooks created by Caroline Fillmore, housed at the Buffalo History Museum. Unfortunately, she neither dated nor marked the source of the many newspaper clippings. But many telling anecdotes came from these.

Chapter One

ABIGAIL'S ROOTS

I WAS THE LAST child born to Rev. Lemuel Powers in March of 1798. Father was a Baptist minister in Stillwater, a small town near Saratoga, New York. His mother, Thankful Leland, was from a prominent New England family—Puritans who had emigrated in 1653. We had the pedigree, but little wealth. I had five elder brothers and a sister Mary, five years older than I; she was my best friend all through our lives. My father died at age 45 when I was just two years old, before I was old enough to appreciate my loss.[1] My mother, born Abigail Newland, thought that the little cash we had would go farther in the wilderness. So we moved to the south end of Owasco Lake of New York's Finger Lakes.

My widowed mother made arrangements to take a wagon train from Albany, travelling 180 miles west, and then south, for Cayuga County in April of 1804. There, in Kelloggsville, we all lived with my older brother Cyrus Powers, 25. He was already established and teaching school.[2]

Our fortunate legacy from my late father was an ample family library. This was the basis of what later became the Powers Library of Moravia, first established around 1818.[3] It was the first of several libraries I had a hand in establishing.

---

[1] Abigail Powers to Solomon Powers, Jan. 25, 1853, Fillmore Papers in SUNY Oswego (FPO)

[2] *Millard Fillmore*, Robert Scarry, 2001

[3] *The Heart of the Fillmore Presidency: Abigail Powers Fillmore and the White House Library*, Elizabeth Lorelei Thacker-Estrada and Frank Severance, *Millard Fillmore Papers*, 1907

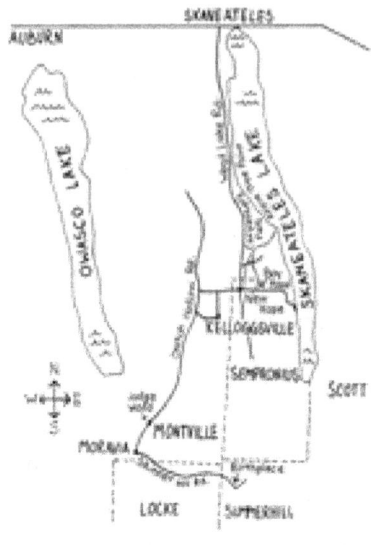

Mother did an excellent job of educating us. I began school at age 6, and discovered a real love of books, music and flowers. Eventually Mother married Benajah Strong. By the age of 16, I had sufficient knowledge to teach summer school, which helped to pay my own winter term tuition in Kelloggsville. By age 19, I taught full time; my brother Cyrus, by then the local judge, thought I could make much more money in needlework or weaving than in teaching school in Sempronius.[4]

My two favorite philosophies reflected my thirst for rigor and for work: "Geography is the science of the earth," and "Industry by habit makes duty a pleasure."[5]

By age 21, I was 5'6" tall with an oval face, high forehead, fair complexion, blue eyes, and light auburn curly hair.[6]

And that was the year my life changed forever.

AT THE brand-new academy opened in Moravia in 1819, I met a tall, young man, who at 19, was also teaching school in Scott and studying at the academy. His name was Millard Fillmore. His face was rugged and handsome, his eyes blue and sparkly, his hair thick and blonde. His family was very poor—just tenant farmers—and he was working hard to help out and to make something of himself. He had very little schooling, learning mostly from his own avid reading.[7]

[4] David Powers to Abigail Powers, Dec. 12, 1817. FPO

[5] Abigail Powers letter, April 13, 1819

[6] *Thirty Years in Washington*, Mrs. John A. Logan, 1901

[7] *The Early Life of Millard Fillmore*, his autobiography, 1871

Abigail's Roots

We found that we shared the goal of pursuing the best education available. What fun we had discussing our books and geographies and our visions for the future.

Millard and I spent many happy hours together studying anything and everything we could. He began to study law under the Quaker judge Walter Wood. I believe this was to please me, which indeed it did. He also completely changed his image--bought a new pair of shoes to replace his cowhide boots, bought a new suit of homespun. He began to wear white collars and to carry a cane. Oh my, he was handsome.

But when his apprenticeship with Judge Wood did not work out, Millard joined his family who had moved west to the little township of Aurora, southeast of Buffalo. Sadly, he carried with him the staggering debt of $65 for the unfinished apprenticeship, a debt that in 1821 seemed insurmountable. His dad, Nathaniel, had finally and happily established his own farm after twenty years of tenant farming. The Fillmore Farm was near the village where Nathaniel's brother Calvin had run the tavern for years.

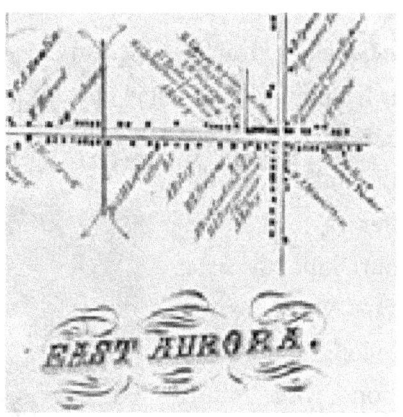

1855 map
Aurora Town Historian's Office

I was sad to see Millard move so far—140 miles away. But he was forlorn and hoping, like Dickens' Micawber, that "something would turn up."[8] He returned to visit me three times—in 1821, 1822 and 1825—always by foot. And we exchanged many, many letters.

---

[8] Micawber was a fictional character in Charles Dickens's novel *David Copperfield*. He is traditionally identified with the optimistic belief that "something will turn up." (Wikipedia)

During the summer of 1824, I moved to Lisle, south of Cortland, NY. My uncle, Herman Powers, had sent for me to educate his three daughters. I was so successful that others asked if I would open a select school. In my year-long endeavor, I was praised as "having a genial spirit, polished manners, good sense, and endowed with fine conversational qualities...an influence at once beneficial and happy."[9]

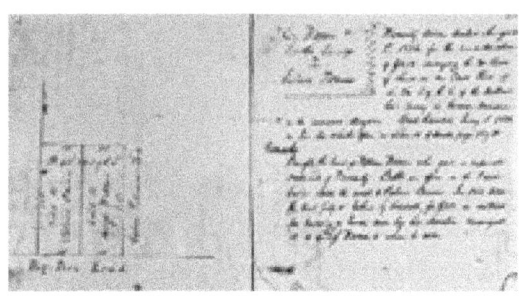

Notes on the purchase of site for law office in 1824, from the notebook of M. Fillmore in Library of Congress

By August of 1824, Millard had saved enough money to build a neat little Greek Revival law office on the north side of Main Street in Aurora, not far from his Uncle Calvin's tavern. During the winter of 1825, after he had succeeded in becoming a lawyer in Buffalo, Millard visited me in Kelloggsville and proposed—after six years of courtship. My sister Mary wrote to me, "I congratulate you upon your future prospects for life... hope that it will increase your happiness. I was as much impressed to hear of his visit, as yourself had not the least expected it...why did

From the author's postcard collection

---

[9] Mary Powers to Abigail Powers, March 6, 1825. Herman Powers to Abigail Fillmore (AF), April 2, 1826, FPO

you not inform me more particularly how he appeared to you and whether you think him improved in etiquette and how Mr. and Mrs. Powers [our brother and his wife] were pleased with him and what remarks they made of him whether he has an introduction…and a hundred other things you omitted writing."[10]

In 1826, to demonstrate his success (in contrast to his many journeys by foot across New York State), Millard took the luxurious stagecoach from the Eagle Tavern on the western edge of Big Tree Road in Willink for the 150-mile trip to Moravia. The stage travelled eastward through Warsaw, Canandaigua, Geneva, and Seneca Falls. The stage rumbled across the nearly mile-long Cayuga Bridge that crossed Cayuga Lake. It was a wooden toll bridge supported upon wooden piles.[11]

On February 26, 1826, we were married in the home of my brother, Judge Cyrus Powers. Rev. Orsanius Smith married us, recording it in his church's records, St. Matthew's Episcopal Church. Mary wrote to me that she was pleased by what she had seen in Millard Fillmore and remarked that "…the thought that you have a kind, affectionate companion whose society will make you more happy than the society of all your friends you have left, at once reconciles me to a separation."[12]

For that time, we were old newlyweds. I was 28—practically a spinster, and Millard was 26, but we had high goals for our lives, and we had been willing to wait for the right time. Some of my family thought I was foolish to marry this son of a tenant farmer, but I believe it worked out just fine.

---

[10] Mary Powers to Abigail Powers, March 6, 1825, FPO

[11] Scarry

[12] Mary Powers to Abigail Fillmore (AF), March 5, 1826, FPO

MARRIAGE IN EAST AURORA

To the town of Aurora we rode[13] to live the first few months with Millard's parents in the farm on Olean Road. That allowed me to continue teaching school, this time at the Aurora village school—even though most women stopped working in those days as soon as they were married.

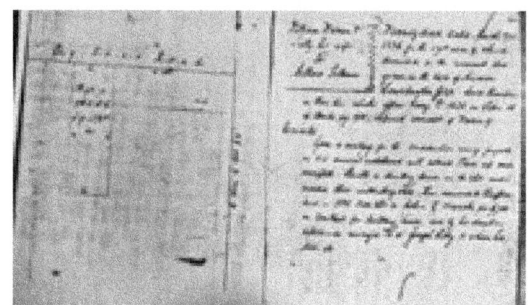

Notes on the purchase of site for house in 1826, from the notebook of M. Fillmore in Library of Congress

I wanted to help Millard achieve all his goals and establish his law practice. So I helped to support him with my earnings, only about $13 a month--$7 in cash and $6 in grain. Little did I know then that simply by teaching after I was married, I would make the record books. I was the first first lady of the White House to work for a salary, to have come from poverty, and to have worked for a living after I was married--even after becoming

---

[13] William E. Griffis, Fillmore Papers, 1:15

a mother. Later, people would call Millard a "wife-made man," because of all my support and educational push.

From the author's postcard collection

In March of 1826, Millard bought the land right across from his law office on the south side of Main Street and began building our little Greek Revival-style home with the help of his many friends and family members. The posts and beams were hand-hewn, with bark still on the timbers. Our home featured clapboard siding, 12 over 8 windows on either side of the front door, four Doric columns—a beautiful little house. We spent many happy hours by the fireplace, studying law and literature, ancient geography maps, and discussing all the fascinating issues of the day. Millard bought books obsessively. Before long, his personal library of 150 books equaled that of the town library, started two years earlier by his uncle Calvin and his friends.

Despite my full life in Aurora, I was a bit homesick. I wrote to my friend Maria Fuller, "Oh, that I may again have the pleasure of spending a happy evening in your family with the little children sitting near me, asking a thousand interesting questions. Would you like to know how I am pleased with the country? It does not appear to me as pleasant as Cayuga, but perhaps it may in time. I enjoy myself as well as I expected to. The inhabitants, as far as I am acquainted, appear friendly."[14]

One of the most fascinating topics that we discussed that year was the mysterious case of William Morgan in Batavia. He had been a printer and a member of the Masons before moving to Batavia, where he applied to

---

[14] AF to Miss Maria Fuller, Aug. 27, 1826, FPO

Marriage in East Aurora

again enter into membership with the Masons.[15]

When his character and history seemed questionable, the lodge members rejected his membership. Morgan then threatened to publish a book, revealing all the secrets of the Masons. Before long, he was jailed and accused of stealing a shirt and necktie. Quickly, Morgan was arrested and hurried by carriage to Canandaigua. Much to the angry Masons' dismay however, Morgan was found innocent by the judge and released for lack of evidence. This was not what the Masons had planned, so they had Morgan re-arrested for a tiny debt of $2, which finally succeeded in having him thrown into prison.

He did not stay there for long, so the story goes. He was said to have been snatched, gagged, tossed into a covered carriage and driven for two days by a shuttling of horses and drivers through Western New York. He finally arrived at Fort Niagara on the tip of Lake Ontario on the evening of September 14th. Friends of Morgan from Batavia were enraged, not knowing what had happened to him. They traveled the fifty miles to Canandaigua, then were sent to Rochester. Through each town that they traveled, the growing story was told. Committees to investigate were formed, but no one could find an answer to the spreading question of "Where's Morgan?"[16]

The Masons were under enormous suspicion since none of them would answer any questions. When the issue was taken to court, the judge, jurors, and sheriff were revealed to be Masons and nothing was done to find the missing Morgan. Cries of "secret societies" and "invisible empire" were drummed up in every town's gossip circles, including the one on Millard's front office step.

Morgan's body was allegedly found more than a year after his disappearance. He had been heavily weighted and thrown overboard into the Niagara River's mouth. His wife Lucinda had to identify his body when it finally washed up onto the shores of Lake Ontario. This outrage spawned a

---

[15] The Masons is the world's largest fraternal organization, whose aim is to promote brotherhood and to foster morality among its members. Because of these events, the Masons wisely abandoned all their political activity after 1832.

[16] *Millard Fillmore: Biography of a President*, by Robert Rayback, 1959

Rochester-based newspaper, *The Antimasonic Enquirer*, edited by Thurlow Weed, who then created an all-out political party, called the Antimasonics.[17] Little did we know what an important and often negative role Mr. Weed would play in our lives.

Nevertheless, at Weed's urging, Millard ventured into politics. He was the perfect candidate in this new era of the Common Man. He was, as were many others, scandalized that anyone could have a higher allegiance to any organization than to American law. He was promptly elected in 1828 as a state assemblyman, representing our growing area in Albany.

And joy of joys, on April 25 of 1828, little Millard Powers Fillmore was born in our home. Named for his father, with my maiden name as his middle, he became known as Powers.

Let me read you a letter I wrote to Millard when he went off to Albany as the State Assemblyman from Aurora:

"I have just received one of the most affectionate letters you have ever written. I was alone and gave vent to my feelings, but I shed no tears of grief. I have been very happy all day, you have been scarcely out of my mind since 7:00 but the perusal of your letter added new energies to my soul and tenderness (if possible) to my heart...."[18]

"I am now alone and having laid our little son on the bed to sleep, I employ a few moments in writing, having again perused your affectionate favor, and to return thanks to kind providence for so tender a friend. Though I regret the loss of your society more than I can express, I am far happier in having you at that distance with an assurance that you love me, than I should be in your society, doubting your affection, but if I could even feel any suspicion your letters are calculated to quiet it all. I contrive to pass away the time as pleasantly as I can...The little boy is well, I mentioned his being out of health the week after you left us, it was probably to cutting teeth; he has now two just cut through the under jaw. I wished last night you could see him after my return; he was wakeful and very interesting. I never saw him more so; he prevented my sleeping nearly an hour with his

---

[17] Rayback

[18] AF to Millard Fillmore (MF), 1/16/1829

innocent and engaging play.[19]

"Although I am sleepy from having been up late several nights past, I could not go quietly to bed without conversing in this silent manner one moment with you. It is your request that I write daily, and I feel it is my greatest pleasure to do so, both because it is your request and because it is more like verbal conversation to communicate the minute transactions of each day and my thought and feelings as they daily occur. I have spent the day at home. Have felt more than usual lonely though not unhappy or discontented. Your society is all I have thought of.

"O, that you could have been here to have studied with me. You have been scarcely out of my mind during the day, soon I hope to have another letter, again peruse the sentiments of my dearest Millerd.[20] I am anxious to have the time come for my soul will then be in happiness. O could I know that you was [sic] happy tonight, and that you felt that confidence in my affection that I do in yours; but you do, you must. I will now bid good night to my kindest and tenderest friend, with the most sincere and ardent wish for his health, happiness, and satisfaction to ever affectionate and devoted Abigail.[21]

"Fearing I shall have no other opportunity tonight, will write one minute now; it is washing day. I have just got my work done and sit down, have been putting on the baby's red shoes, his others are worn out. I wish you were here to see him maneuver. He laughs and stamps and plays with his shoes. I wish you could read to me as you frequently have done after I sit down to sewing.[22]

"The family have all retired to rest except myself. I have nothing to inform you of but little family occurrences, those I believe may be interesting, if I can judge of your feelings by your writing. I have spent the day at home, working on my veil. Nathan has this evening read part of a play in Shakespeare, it was *The Two Gentlemen of Verona*. Doubtless you recollect

---

[19] Ibid, Jan. 17th, 11:00 p.m.

[20] 19th century spellings were notably fluid.

[21] AF to MF, Jan. 18th, Sunday evening, 10:00 p.m.

[22] Ibid, Jan. 19th, 3:00 p.m.

what confidence the fair Julia placed in her Proteus, who fell in love with Silvia. I could not but reflect upon the liability of a changing man's affections, in seeing a new or fairer object, although you are separated from me by a greater distance and daily behold fairer and more accomplished females than her who has the good fortune to be bound to you by the strongest and most delicate of nature. I still am happy and proud in the thought that your heart is firm, and that no fascinating female can induce you to forget her whose whole heart is devoted and who will continue to count the days until you are again restored to her arms. Good night, my Millerd, a thousand blessings is upon you, may you sleep sweetly with the image of your Abigail hovering over you like a guardian sphinx."[23]

The next night I wrote, "It is a fine day but rather too warm for the snow, we have had elegant sleighing for several days, but I fear we shall lose it. A few more hours and I shall know whether I can hear from you. I know not why I am so anxious to receive a letter. I will not be foolish even if I do not receive one today; perhaps you are engaged in business and I will excuse you, that Heaven may release my Millerd, is the ardent wish of his affectionate Abigail."[24]

Millard wrote back: "...were it not for the business that occupies my mind I sincerely believe that I should be homesick beyond endurance. I wish you were here, for I have no female society, and no friends with whom I can sympathize in this hour of affliction. All the satisfaction I have is in writing to and hearing from those who are absent…I attend no places of amusement but spend all my time in business…."[25]

I did help Millard with a naming task. The state wanted to rename Erie, New York, to distinguish it from Erie, Pennsylvania. I had just been reading the works of Lord George Byron, so I suggested the name "Newstead" to match Byron's ancestral home. Thus was Newstead, New York, named by me.[26]

---

[23] Ibid, Jan. 20th, 11:00 p.m.

[24] Ibid, Jan. 22nd

[25] MF to AF via Mary Powers at Kelloggsville, Feb. 19, 1830, FPO

[26] Thomas McKaig, "Place Names of Western New York"

Chapter Three

WIDENING WORLD IN THE THIRTIES

By 1830, Millard felt ready to join the Big Boys, the established lawyers in Buffalo. He commissioned a simple, two-story, six-room Federal white clapboard house at 114 [now 180]²⁷ Franklin St., a mere two blocks from Main Street. For the next twenty years Millard and I happily raised our family there.

From <u>Picture Book of Earlier Buffalo</u> by Frank Severance

The exterior had "two Doric columns, topped by a frieze… and a widow's walk on the flat roof."²⁸ It had green shutters and a center hall entrance

---

²⁷ *Picture Book of Earlier Buffalo*, Frank Severance, ed., 16:384.

²⁸ Charles Snyder, *The Lady and the President: The Letters of Dorothea Dix and Millard Fillmore*, p. 32

with a staircase framed with a rosewood banister. On the left was our library, ready to fill with our collection of books.

Finally, I felt financially comfortable enough to discontinue my teaching. I taught myself to speak French, took up piano-playing, and read avidly. Our library soon held four thousand books. I freely called for the carpenter to add bookcases whenever we needed more shelf space.[29]

I was very conversant on all the issues that Millard had to face. But Millard never took an important step without consulting me first, He often remarked that he could never destroy any of my letters, even the little notes I sent to his office.

Buffalo had become a wild and interesting boomtown, Queen City of the Lakes. Wrapped in blankets, native Americans walked the muddy, unpaved streets in their moccasins. Pigs roamed wild, cows grazed on front yards. Millard built me a white picket fence and I busily cultivated one of the most beautiful flower gardens in Buffalo. We planted lilacs and Japanese quince bushes in the front yard. We had arrived.

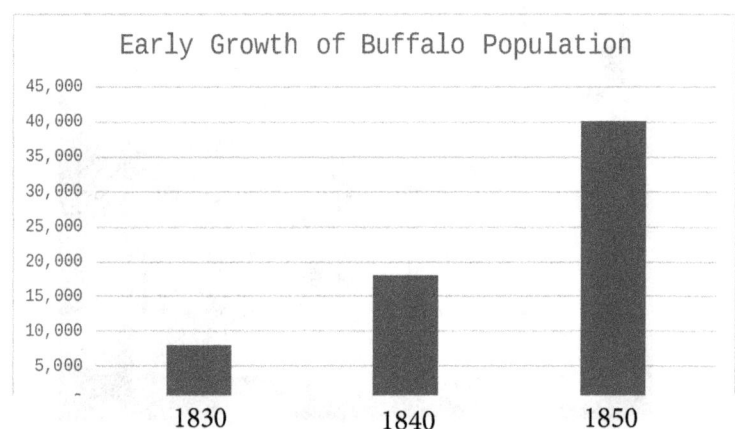

Because the canal and harbor were frozen and empty, the whole city of Buffalo partied all winter. Oh, Millard was such a charmer! I was the envy of all the women. We attended Shakespearean plays at the Eagle Street Theatre, chamber music recitals, and even heard Horace Greeley speak. We joined the Lyceum and heard formal debates, collected rocks and plants,

---

[29] Fillmore Papers, 2:596

conducted chemistry and physics experiments. In 1831, my husband and I were charter members of the new Unitarian Church in Buffalo. Pushing for public schools, Buffalo offered the first public free elementary schools in the state; Millard helped to incorporate Buffalo as a city in 1832.[30]

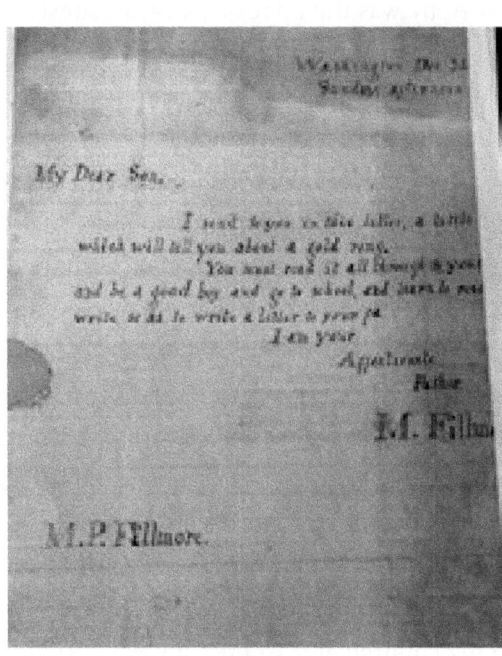

Collection of The Buffalo History Museum. Millard Fillmore Papers, Mss. C79-1, Box 1, Folder 3.

On March 27, 1832, my daughter Mary Abigail was born; we called her Abby. But that summer we followed the newspaper reports of the advance of cholera from Europe to Quebec, and down the St. Lawrence to Little York.[31] 3500 people died of it in New York City, 5000 in New Orleans in two weeks. Finally, it hit Buffalo in July and claimed 200 people.[32] We packed up Powers and Abby and moved out to East Aurora for the summer to live with Grandfather Nathaniel.[33]

Millard became a popular and successful lawyer, elected three times to the State Assembly, and four times—'32, '36, '38 and '40--to Congress.

---

[30] *The Buffalo Republican*, a newspaper from 1828-1835

[31] Now Toronto

[32] It would be thirty more years before scientists learned that cholera was caused by unclean water, flies, and dirty hands. Germ theory had not yet been discovered. The treatment at that time for cholera was a mix of equal parts tincture of opium, red pepper, rhubarb, essence of peppermint and spirits of camphor. Sometimes women even wore little bags of this mixture around their necks and hidden under their clothes as a preventative measure

[33] Millard's mother Phoebe had died in May of 1831.

Bringing up my children was my focus. Millard was a wonderful father. I have a letter he wrote from Washington to five-year-old Powers, in December of 1833 (see box on p. 25).

Powers was powerfully shy. We had to coax him to enter any room with anyone other than family.[34] But Abby was the opposite, a ray of sunshine from the beginning.

In 1836, I was on my way to Washington--by stage to Pittsburgh, a steamboat to Wheeling, by railroad to Harpers Ferry and by water on the Chesapeake and Ohio Canal to Georgetown. I described Pittsburgh to my eight-year-old Powers, who with his sister was staying with my sister Mary: "The city is very dirty, the houses are black and smokey*[sic]* on account of their burning so much coal and all the children looked as if they played in blacksmith shops."[35]

I was picky about how Powers wrote letters back to me, telling him he should take pains with his letter writing, practice on slate first with words he was unsure of in spelling, hold his pen correctly, place his capital letters in the correct place, be aware of punctuation, date letters with name of place and spell all the words correctly. However, I felt his letters were well written and that writing was a great accomplishment.[36] When I was not at home, I expected a letter from my children at least once a week, certainly every Sunday.

When Abby still five, I complimented her on her neat letter. I did point out that her o's appeared more like a's. However, I could not believe that she had written the letter with no mistakes in spelling. Aunt Mary wrote on the bottom of Abby's letter as a PS that Abby had composed it by herself.[37]

In 1837, with Powers 10 and Abby 6, they were old enough to be left with their grandparents or Aunt Mary in East Aurora or Aunt Julia in Buffalo. I could travel to DC for longer periods of time alone. How I loved the wealth

---

[34] Memorial Meeting for Powers Fillmore of the Erie County Bar Asso., 1890

[35] AF to Abby, May 12, 1836

[36] AF to Powers, 1837

[37] AF to Abby, Dec. 5, 1837, FPO

My Widening World in the Thirties

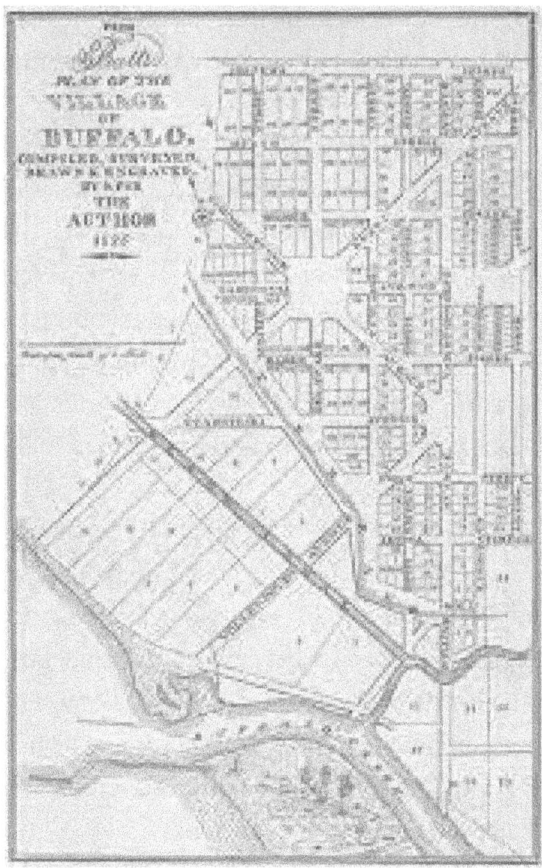

From History of Buffalo *by Sheldon Ball*

of culture available to me now! I attended an interesting lecture by an Englishman in Washington on Egypt concerning Alexandria, the Nile, and Thebes. With Powers, I went to a Chinese museum in Philadelphia.[38]

In June of 1838, I visited the Capitol to hear lively debates in the Senate, including one by Henry Clay. The ladies in the Senate sat behind a railing which enclosed them, and the men were in a reserved section of the gallery above them.

In early December of 1837, Abby and I made our way to Washington. At Albany, we boarded the *Swallow*, then the fastest steamboat on the Hudson for the six-hour trip to NYC. I had Powers trace our trip on a map. From New York to Baltimore we covered 215 miles in fourteen hours. On a steamboat at Philadelphia were twenty Indian chiefs from the West with colorful feathers and painted faces…They departed at Baltimore. We took a fast train from Baltimore to Washington—one mile in three minutes.

But all was not excitement and trips and lectures. My mother, Abigail Newland Powers, died on February 23, 1838, at nearly 80 years of age. "You know not how it affects your Ma to hear your dear Grandma is dead…. I

---

[38] Ibid, June 7, 1840

did not go to sleep last night until one o'clock for weeping. I wish I could have seen her once more, but I never can now. I have no dear kind mother and you have no dear grandmother."[39]

By early May of 1838, we were on the road again. Six-year-old Abby and I took a boat ride on Chautauqua Lake. She was frightened by the noise of the steamboat.[40] In June, I visited the War Department and saw over 100 portraits of the American Indian, including Red Jacket from Western New York. I left my cards at several heads of departments and foreign ministers. At the State Department, I viewed official government seals of countries that had diplomatic relations with the United States and presents from foreign rulers to our ministers. The original copy of the Declaration of Independence was also on display.[41]

Ten-year-old Powers wrote to us from his grandparents' home in East Aurora, commenting, "There was plenty of sleighing and skating this winter," the same winter he had learned to skate.[42] In Washington, we were struck by a rain and sleet storm. The roads, sidewalks and ground were covered with a thick, smooth coating of ice. From a window in Mrs. Pitman's boarding house, I saw a boy about my son's size skating, and he had a severe fall. I thought of my own son, if he had bought new skates and wondered if he had any bad falls during the winter.[43]

Young Abby wrote her father of New Year's Day at Buffalo in 1839. "The table was decorated with red and green flowers and had everything on it— Mother's candy, all kinds of cake, whip cream, little crackers, grapes, onions, and a great many other things. We received calls, but I did not enjoy myself, because Ma kept me cooped up in the house all day with her to see company."[44]

Powers proved to be a good student. "In arithmetic, I was hopeful that

---

[39] AF to Abby, March 8, 1838

[40] AF to MF, May 18, 1838

[41] AF to Mary Powers for Abby, June 17, 1838

[42] Powers to Dear Pa and Ma, March 4, 1838

[43] AF to Powers, Feb. 18, 1838

[44] Abby to MF, Jan. 2, 1839 FPO

my ten-year-old son was able to solve division problems…"[45] By fourteen, "I was delighted in my son's progress. I told him, 'I remember that no study ever pleased me like arithmetic, altho' my opportunity for indulging my task were limited in comparison to yours."[46]

When Powers was eleven, staying with his grandparents in East Aurora, I advised him, "If you wish more spending money, ask your grandpa to let you have some on your pa's account, but you must try to spend it judiciously. Write to me everything you bought, that I may see how you have used your money. When you wish to buy anything, ask your grandpa always if he thinks best, and do as he says."[47]

The elder Fillmores had horses, a cow, pet rabbits, and various dogs. I made sure that Abby had private tutors for modern languages, music, drawing and painting.

In the summer of 1839, our family went to Saratoga Springs for its healing waters and resort life. We had delightful rooms, but because my foot was ailing me, I didn't feel well, and the waters made it worse. Abby drank the water but didn't like it. She had some lemonade from High Rock Spring, the most popular spring.[48] Millard also visited Sharon Springs near Albany but found the water "sulphorous" and "loathsome to the taste," yet managed a "single tumble full."[49] Not all our new experiences were rapturous.

---

[45] AF to Powers, March 15, 1838 FPO

[46] AF to Powers, June 5, 1842

[47] AF to Powers, May 19, 1841

[48] Abby to Powers, July 26, 1839

[49] MF to AF, May 11, 1848

THE FORTIES

Our whole family evolved in so many ways during the 1840s. Powers ultimately followed his father into law, attending the Law School in Albany, then Harvard Law School in Cambridge. He eventually returned to clerk in Millard's law office.

State Normal School
From the author's postcard collection

Abby, my darling daughter, studied French, German, Italian, and Spanish with private tutors; she mastered drawing, painting, piano, harp and guitar. She was personable and responsible--an ideal daughter in every way. Abby followed my example by graduating from the State Normal School and becoming a teacher in Buffalo.

I loved flowers; I had a conservatory added to my Buffalo home so I could have flowers summer and winter. When I was absent from my Buffalo home, I remained concerned about my plants. I wondered in particular about a rose bush I left in the care of my 14-year-old Powers. He wrote that the flowers looked very well, the rose bush had a blossom, as did a horseshoe geranium.[50]

My friend, Mrs. Solomon Havens, observed "…what was peculiar [to Millard was] the marked courtesy of manner with which he always addressed Mrs. Fillmore and the polite attention which he accorded her. It was like that which a man usually bestows upon a guest. I remember, at a party at my own house one cold winter night, that after escorting Mrs. Fillmore to the parlor, he quietly slipped away to his own home, returning to surprise her with the flowers she had cut from her own conservatory and carefully arranged, but had forgotten to bring with her. It was these small attentions, so natural to him, that gave a distinctive mark to the daily intercourse of their lives. Mrs. Fillmore was a woman who had read much and who was well informed upon all the topics of the day, and Mr. Fillmore had the highest respect for her attainments, and has been heard to say that he never took any important step without her counsel and advice."[51]

Millard wrote to me every day that we were not together in Washington—except when he also served as Chairman of Ways and Means—then he wrote every other day.[52]

Sewing was one of my passions. I would make clothing—a dress, apron, bonnet, jacket, shawl and more for myself and my daughter. I also did mounds of mending. From the age of five, Abby was knitting and sewing. At six, Abby finished a bed quilt. Later, when she was at school in Lenox, I would send her garments I had made, as well as material and patterns for her to sew. When Millard was comptroller at Albany, I encouraged Abby to bring her sewing with her when she stayed with us. If a problem developed, I would send Abby to a dressmaker.

---

[50] Powers to AF, May 22, 1842, FPO

[51] Mrs. Solomon Haven, BECHS

[52] Caroline's Scrapbook

I could speak and translate some French while also encouraging my children to pursue the study of a foreign language. Powers began French and German at age eleven and by fourteen, Latin. Abby began French at eight, German and Latin at fifteen.

From the author's postcard collection

The Erie Canal became more and more important to us in Buffalo. I travelled it in late spring of 1841, but was not fond of the crowded conditions of the packet boat. The first day we had eighteen ladies and seven children; the second day, there were twenty ladies and eleven children and gentlemen without number.[53] I traveled to Old Salt Road in Kelloggsville near Skaneateles Lake by canal, and then by lumber wagon to visit my sick older brother Cyrus. He had helped to raise me after our father passed when I was two.[54] Now his feet were gangrened, and he sadly died at the age of 62 in October of 1841.

Throughout the years when Millard was in Washington as a congressman, I would occasionally stay with him for months at a time. We would leave Buffalo late in the year, and I would remain in DC until spring. Other years, I would leave in the spring for the nation's capital and return to Buffalo in the autumn before winter set in. Sometimes Abby would accompany me. I was fortunate to have my sister Mary as a surrogate mother.

From Washington in 1841, nine-year-old Abby wrote her brother from our boarding house "…three men came in to play harps. We dressed, went

---

[53] AF to MF, May 17, 1841

[54] Ibid

downstairs, and danced and waltzed to their music."⁵⁵ But when she was stuck in Washington in 1842, ten-year-old Abby was anxious to go home. I had promised her that she could have a small room over the porch for a playhouse or theatre. Abby thought she was too big for a playhouse and intended it to be the latter. She hoped that her brother would be an actor in it.⁵⁶

I wrote to Powers, "The months of June and July in DC were difficult for young Abby. It was so warm and hot at the end of June, that she couldn't wear calico and gingham dresses. She wished that she were in Buffalo even for five minutes—a lake breeze would have been a luxury…In July, sweat ran off her face in large drops, making it difficult to write."⁵⁷

A frequent House observer, I wrote to Powers, "the House did not adjourn today until 6 o'clock and we were half starved, having eaten nothing since breakfast at 8 o'clock."⁵⁸

In 1842, Powers wrote us on a Sunday. It had been a rainy day and he didn't go to church. He had read all day. I admonished him: "I wish you would go to church always at least once on every Sunday. It is right to go to church, besides it is better for your health than to read all day."⁵⁹

When Abby remained in Buffalo, she would stay with her grandparents in East Aurora or with her Aunt Mary in Lodi, Ludlowville (Lansing), or La Grange (Irving), NY. Her brother usually remained in East Aurora with his grandparents. On other occasions, my sister Mary or Fillmore's sister would take care of both at their home in Buffalo.⁶⁰

During the fall of 1844, Powers lent a friend his shotgun. He and his companion walked to East Aurora, "hunting all the way through the

---

[55] Abby to Powers, June 18, 1841.

[56] Abby to Powers, July 21, 1842

[57] Abby to Powers, June & July, 1841

[58] AF to Powers, June 1841

[59] AF to Powers, April 18, 1842

[60] Scarry

woods.⁶¹ At his grandfather's farm, game was plentiful, such as woodchucks and partridges."⁶²

From the collection of the Genesee Country Village & Museum

I wrote to Powers, asking if he remembered his sister's birthday, reminding him that in four weeks it would be his own birthday. "It seems but a few days since you was [sic] but an infant in my arms and in a few days more, you will have grown to manhood…You will wonder at the rapidity of time, and perhaps may sometimes regret that you have not spent it to better ad-

---

⁶¹ "Powers is portrayed in an oil painting by artist Nelson Cook, nattily attired in a jacket and tie with a double-barreled percussion cap shotgun, glass powder flask, leather holder for two kinds of shot, eyeglass and a dog." Genesee Country Village and Museum

⁶² Powers to MF, Oct. 23, 1844, FPO

vantage. Not that you will have cause to do so, my son, more than others, but everyone does, more or less and we only learn by experience our errour [sic] that a great part of our own life has been actually wasted..."[63]

To Powers on his 14th birthday: "...how short the time seems since your birth! What changes will have taken place before another fourteen years has fled—should you be spared to see that time, both your parents may be sleeping in the silent grave. I wish you not to anticipate grief, it will come fast enough, and I think it a duty to cultivate cheerfulness of heart—and I will change the subject."[64]

Millard remained ever the attentive husband. In a trip in early April, he wrote to me from the Eagle Tavern in Rochester, where he had stayed for the night before going home by way of Canandaigua. He was upset that he was going to be detained one day in reaching home: "I want to see you very much. I have much to tell that I cannot write. But you shall know all when I see you...My love to Mary and the children. I am as ever all your own and only yours—Millard."[65]

On July 4 of 1842, I slipped on an uneven surface of a sidewalk and turned my foot inward. The next day, my foot became inflamed and swollen.[66] By January, my foot had improved, but then worsened. Millard wrote that I exert myself too much; he was apprehensive that I will never be well unless I keep still.[67] He wrote to Powers, "Ma's foot is worse again. I feel very anxious about it. I fear she will not be able to walk before I come home. How much she has suffered."[68]

In July of 1844, I visited the Avon Springs, southwest of Rochester, and poured warm water on my bad foot in the evening and cold water in the morning.[69] And thus began the end of my easy mobility.

---

[63] AF to Powers, March 27, 1842, FPO

[64] AF to Powers, April 25, 1842

[65] MF to AF, April 9, 1844, FPO

[66] AF to Powers, July 10, 1842

[67] MF to Powers, Feb. 4, 1843

[68] MF to Powers, Feb. 17, 1843

[69] AF to Abby, July 28, 1844

The Forties

In April of 1845, I wrote to C.F. Perkins: "My foot gained as fast as I could reasonably expect and the latter part of the last summer, I was enabled to lay aside my crutches, only bearing my weight upon the heel of the foot. I have continued to gain ever since, though not yet well. My foot is weak and tender to the bone and gives me some pain in walking, though less and less every month.

"I am confident there is a great similarity in our cases…the pain seemed to be most on the outer side of the instep and through the back part of the foot below the ankle joint. I immediately called a physician. He decided that the outer bone of the ankle was cracked, but did not think any ligament was ruptured. After two weeks' time, I began to walk on it, although it was very weak and lame.

"I used the oil of Origanian (or nisser), used it too plentifully. This together with over-exercise and perhaps a little cold injured my foot, and it became seriously inflamed…I was confined to my bed nearly the whole autumn and to my room many months after. The inflammation was greatest in the lower part of the foot, and for many months it would be necessary to open it on the ball of the foot under the great toe joint.

"The inflammation however gradually subsided, but it could bear no weight upon it or suffer it to remain long in a pendant position—and for two years any excitement or muscular exertion would produce pain and inflammation. The more quiet I was, the more comfortable my foot would be and generally, I slept tolerably well the latter part of the night. It would however require some hours of perfect quiet before my foot would become easy enough to sleep.

"My physician told me the inflammation was in the vessels and membrane which covers the bone and between the joints and that it would require a long time of rest for the inflammation to subside."[70]

However, I could still work at my crafts. At the sixth annual Cattle Show and Fair of the NYS Agricultural Society held in Auburn on September 15-17 of 1846, I submitted a needle and wax work, plus an ornamental

---

[70] April 17, 1845

bead bell rope. The Committee on Ornamental Shells awarded me $5 and a diploma.[71]

Once the railroad to western New York was completed in 1840, Niagara Falls became the summer resort for the whole country; many famous people stopped by our home in Buffalo. In October of 1843, we entertained John Quincy Adams, the former president and now an esteemed congressman. We had a small circle of friends over to meet Mr. Adams and we all enjoyed a remarkable conversation. He also accompanied us to services at our Unitarian church. Adams left with this compliment: "Millard Fillmore was one of the ablest, most faithful and fairest men with whom it has been my lot to serve in public life."[72]

We received an invitation to attend a gathering of the great family of Lelands—my father's Puritan line—at Saratoga in New York State, "creating more than ordinary feelings in both of us." All due preparations were made, and the time for departure arrived. Millard was 45 or 46 years of age at that time, in the pride of manly beauty; I was a year or two his senior, but no one would have suspected it, as I then appeared in the very perfection of womanhood. The prestigious Leland family numbered several thousand, and there were between one and two thousand who made their appearance

Grand Ball in Saratoga, NY

---

[71] NYS Agricultural Society, 1846, 6, 102

[72] John Robert Irelan, *History of the Life, Administration, and Times of Millard Fillmore*

in that assembly. It would have been an inspiring scene for a painter to mark our entry into that congregation, with the glow of triumph on our cheeks. After my family had disapproved of marrying Millard, it was sweet to enter the ball on his arm. A newspaper of 1848 described my husband: "His walk has the freedom of an Indian, his face the honesty of the farmer, his brain the intellect of a scholar and his manners the polish of a gentleman. He has carved out his fortune with no other aid than his own resolute will, his own strong intellect and his own untiring energy."

Millard Fillmore's name was a household word in most of the families of this state, and in that assembly, he was voted the "noblest Roman of them all." For a long time afterwards, that trip furnished a favorite subject for conversation by the firesides for both of us.[73]

---

[73] Hiram Day, BECHS, p. 506

Chapter Five

A STINT IN ALBANY AND BACK TO DC

Aside from the growing turmoil over slavery--between those who would enslave and those who wanted slavery abolished--the political world of the 1840s was treacherous. My husband served as the Chairman of the Ways and Means Committee, a reward from his dedicated service to the Whig party. But at the 1844 Whig convention in Baltimore, our old friend and supporter Thurlow Weed began to turn against Millard. Weed blocked Fillmore's chance to run as vice-president by having Millard nominated for governor of New York. Millard was, as they say, a "sacrificial lamb" for the governor position, because everyone knew that a Whig could not win that race. It was the first time my dear husband ever lost an election.[74]

Weed later patched things up with an arrangement for Millard to win the New York state comptroller position, the first person ever elected to this important job. This put him in charge of the state's finances, which, flooded with payments from the lucrative Erie Canal, was a daunting assignment. He won this election with the largest vote any New York Whig had ever received.

Millard sold his law books to his partner Solomon Haven, who served in 1847 as the mayor of Buffalo; they closed the very profitable law firm of Fillmore, Hall and Haven. Our children were both at school in Massachusetts—Powers at Harvard and Abby at Lenox. Due to frequent migraines and my foot troubles, my declining health was too poor to be troubled with

---

[74] Rayback, p. 160

the cares of housekeeping in Albany. We looked for a temperance house to avoid the constant rush and bustle that would disturb my need for quiet and repose, hoping my health would improve. Alas, we ended up at Delevan House on Broadway, between Steuben and Columbia Streets, where there was dancing every evening in the parlor.

From the collection of the Aurora Historical Society

Abby's piano was shipped by Erie Canal from Buffalo to Albany.[75] She was attending the private school of Mrs. Charles Sedgwick at Lenox, Massachusetts on Kemble St., opposite the Trinity Episcopal Church. Many daughters of famous people were educated at Mrs. Sedgwick's, including Ralph Waldo Emerson's daughter Ellen and Jennie Jerome.[76] Our letters were full of concerns for her studies. I told her to read no more novels, but to concentrate on more useful instruction books. At the end of the summer of 1848, her father sent Abby a large basket of fresh peaches and hoped that she and her "companions had a feast."

I advised her to "be careful in speaking freely before others who may misrepresent your views. Let it be a lesson to be more reserved…endeavor to be amiable and obliging. I am sure you would be so if you could control your feelings."[77] Having finished Mrs. Sedgwick's, Abby felt the necessity of attaining an academic education, not merely of grace and ornament, but one that would allow her an ability to support herself.

From Albany, it was easier for Millard and me to visit Saratoga Springs

---

[75] AF to Abby, Dec. 19, 1847

[76] Scarry—Jerome was the mother of Winston Churchill

[77] AF to Abby, March 24, 1848, FPO

and the Eastern Seaboard. When Powers was at Cambridge and Abby at Lenox, I occasionally enjoyed journeying to Boston.[78] I also tried riding all night from Buffalo to Albany in one of the new railroad night cars. I enjoyed the seats with high backs, arms, cushions to keep heads from rolling out and seat cushions as soft as a rocking chair so one could sleep well.[79]

For the summer of 1848, Millard traveled by boat from NYC to Newport, Rhode Island, to find a spot--the Ocean House on Bellevue Ave--for me to stay the summer. He then returned to Albany for his comptroller duties. Powers and I enjoyed bathing in the surf at the beach a mile away[80] and horseback riding, but I was lonely and homesick. "The crowd is greater than it was at Saratoga last summer and very gay and fashionable. It is amusing to look on and see the great variety of costume, and the great effort made to rival each other at display in dress."[81] Millard stayed just a few days on weekends, commuting back to Albany.

Abby's next step after Lenox was to attend the State Normal School in Buffalo to qualify for a teaching position.[82] At age 17, Abby received her diploma after six months and began teaching.[83]

Millard and I enjoyed the social life in Albany, such as the party given by Solomon Van Rensselaer. It was "very splendid—that is the rooms were large and handsomely fitted up and brilliantly lighted with gas and a great display of dress."[84] In Albany, I heard a singing group called the Hutchinsons. I wrote to Abby that they were not "extraordinary and I didn't like their selection of songs. Their greatest charm is their singing so naturally and uneffectually [sic]."[85] Our usual letter topics were much more serious ones—the abolition of slavery, temperance, and women's rights. Our

---

[78] AF to Abby, Sept. 24, 1848, FPO

[79] AF to Abby, Aug. 18, 1848

[80] MF to Abby, Aug. 11, 1848

[81] AF to Abby, Aug. 6 & 20, 1848

[82] Caroline's scrapbook

[83] Abby to MF, June 9, 1849

[84] MF to Abby, Jan. 18, 1848

[85] AF to Abby, Sept. 24, 1848

lives changed abruptly and radically after the Whig convention in 1848. Whig boss Thurlow Weed made sure the nominee for president was General Zachary Taylor, a war hero who had never even voted. But the Whig convention could not decide on who should share the ticket with Taylor. Finally, John Collier of Binghamton rose, and out of the blue, nominated Millard.[86] His logic was that since Taylor was from the South with over a hundred slaves, the Whigs needed to balance the ticket with a vice president from the North who could bring people together. Millard won the nomination in only two ballots, infuriating Weed who had wanted his new favorite, Willliam Seward, as vice president.[87]

After their successful election, Millard resigned from Comptroller of New York State in February of 1849. He stayed in Washington at the Willard Hotel at 14th and Pennsylvania Avenue, then moving to the Irving House.[88] I was less than thrilled and did not even go to Washington for his inauguration. Neither Mrs. Taylor nor I attended the inauguration or the three inaugural balls.

A strange quirk of history happened due to the usual inauguration date falling on a Sunday, moving inauguration to Monday, March 5th. James Polk's term finished on Saturday, leaving the country officially without a leader for one day.

Personally, I was going through a difficult time, depressed over the recent serious sickness of my beloved sister Mary. I had experienced a strong premonition that I would not have too many more birthdays. I wrote to Millard… "perhaps ere another anniversary I shall be numbered with the dead--I feel a pre-sentiment that I shall not see many more."[89]

And why wouldn't I think of my own mortality? All my brothers but one had already died--in 1821, '30, '35, '41. I was deeply worried for Mary especially. Almost all my birth family gone but me. I wrote daily to Millard though, and he visited me as often as possible.

---

[86] Caroline's scrapbook

[87] Rayback, p. 148 & 186

[88] There was no official vice-presidential residence.

[89] AF to MF, March 14, 1849

A Stint in Albany and Back to DC

From Albany I wrote, "I pity you, and am glad I am not there in the evening as lame as I am now. I am no better, but worse than I wrote you last. My lameness is in one hip…I have suffered a great deal of pain this week, and cannot stand on my feet…today am much worse…I keep watch of the proceedings at Washington, for I have taken to reading newspapers since you left…I shall think of you tomorrow, I hope no accident will happen in the crowd…."[90]

I made plans to leave Albany for Buffalo in spring of 1849. "I wish I could see you, when shall I have that pleasure? I am much better for two or three days past, not in much pain if I keep quiet, though I am still very lame."[91]

In June Millard returned home, stopping in NYC and West Point. At the Military Academy he received a 17-gun salute by the Cadet battery in honor of his arrival. That June we together visited our old home of Cayuga County, enjoying Millard's new status as the Vice President of the United States.

Powers graduated from Harvard University with a degree in law on July 18, 1849. Powers wrote to his sister, "I am putting Father to a great deal of expense and whether I shall ever be benefitted by it enough to repay him, time only can tell."[92]

He began a law partnership in Buffalo with William H. Andrews. Abby was then teaching in the common schools in Buffalo.[93] My heart was certainly in Buffalo, but by December of 1849 we were back in DC.

I left Washington for Buffalo at the end of March of 1850. Millard wrote to me, "How lonesome this room is in your absence…How I wish I could be with you! I want to see the children very much…I have no one to play backgammon with…and have only room enough left to say what you very well know, that I am your own devoted Millard."[94]

---

[90] AF to MF, March 1 & 2, 1849

[91] AF to MF, March 11, 1849, FPO

[92] Powers to AF, April 19, 1849, FPO

[93] MF to Wm. Scott, Nov. 8, 1849

[94] MF to AF, April 1, 1850

But disaster struck in 1850. On July 4th, at the Washington Monument, President Taylor listened to the long orations with his head uncovered on a broiling hot day and suffered a sunstroke, overcome with the heat. When he was somewhat revived, he ate cherries and drank ample iced water and milk, but became critically ill with a high fever. (Other accounts named cucumbers, cabbage, wild berries, and bread.) By any account, he was overcome with cholera morbus and died in five days.

Powers's sheepskin diploma, written in Latin—an artifact of the Aurora Historical Society

Chapter Six

POLITICAL PITFALLS OF 1850

The President and his wife! How could this be? We were the first presidential couple to have risen from abject poverty to this auspicious position. Millard prayed fervently for wisdom, as this was a most divided and volatile time for the still young nation. Taylor's Cabinet made it worse by resigning *en masse*. Millard asked them for a month of transition; they gave him a week.

*As vice president, Fillmore oversaw the debate of the Clay Compromise.
From the collection of the Aurora Historical Society*

Millard wrote, "The country seemed on the verge of revolution…I soon saw that I must rely upon myself and act for myself, that the country was in peril, that I was bound to sacrifice everything, even life itself, to save it. I resolved that the Constitution should be my chart…that I would not suffer Her to be plunged into the breakers by the abolitionists of the North or the disunionists of the South…."[95]

As vice president, my husband had presided over the contentious debate over Henry Clay's compromise proposal. California, flush with residents because of the Gold Rush, was petitioning to skip the usual stage of being a territory and to join the Union directly as a state. Gold miners did not want slavery in their state because they wanted to harvest the gold on their own. And what was to be of the territory won by the Mexican-American War—should they be slave or free, and who would decide? The main concession to the South in this Compromise was that the already extant Fugitive Slave Law was to be given enforceable teeth. Zachary Taylor wanted no part of the compromise; it was on this vast tension that Taylor left all these complexities to Millard.

Let me be clear. I stayed informed on all these issues and certainly had opinions. I felt my main role in the White House was to provide counsel and advice for Millard. I was a lifelong opponent of slavery, as was Millard. Writing to Daniel Webster, Millard confessed, "God knows that I detest slavery, but it is an existing evil…and we must endure it and give it such protection as is guaranteed by the Constitution, until we can get rid of it without destroying the last hope of free government in the world."[96] [97]

But Millard made his own decisions. People say I advised him not to sign the Compromise, but I never put that in writing.

Millard later reflected that signing the Fugitive Slave Law in September of 1850 was the most painful act of his life.[98] He had submitted the pro-

---

[95] MF to My Dear Cousin, 1851

[96] MF Papers, Letter to Webster, Oct. 1850

[97] Rayback, p. 252

[98] Caroline's scrapbook

posed law to the Attorney General to determine its constitutionality and it had been approved to be so. His dream was peace—to preserve, without hatred and without war, tranquility throughout the length and breadth of our land.[99]

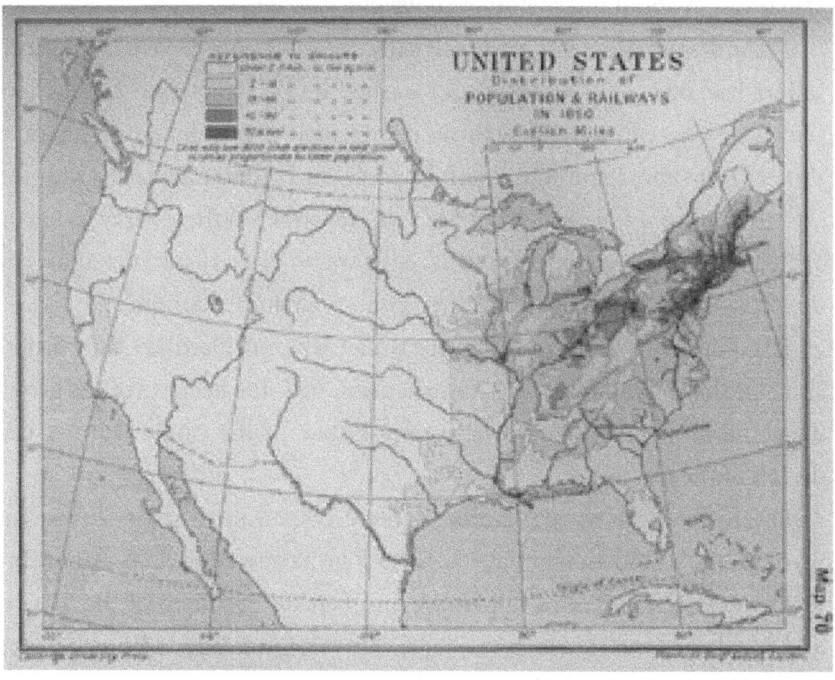

From the Cambridge Modern History Atlas, 1912.

He believed that, had he not signed, the southern states would have seceded immediately, and the North was not yet ready for such a war. Millard was consciously choosing to keep the country together and to follow the Constitution. He and most other Americans at the time saw slavery as a legal issue, less so a moral issue.

I would also like to point to several other accomplishments of his two and a half years in office. Millard knew that it was important to get cross-continental railroads built to California. He had "…deep interest in any project calculated to facilitate the intercommunication between the Atlantic and

---

[99] Gen. J. Grant Wilson, Jan. 1878

Pacific states. If we cannot bind those states to us by roads, railroads, and telegraph lines, we may soon see them setting up for independence...."[100]

Under Fillmore's presidency, the price of postage actually went down. A single letter cost three cents when prepaid, five when sent "on credit." He also brought about international copyright.

Millard had problems in the Pacific to solve too. Several American sailors had been ship-wrecked and washed up on Japanese shores, where they were treated poorly. The President decided to negotiate with Japan to protect our sailors and to open their ports for commercial trade with the U.S. In November of 1852, Fillmore sent Admiral Matthew Perry to Japan, armed with full negotiation powers. Four warships were instructed to rendezvous in the Chinese Sea and then go into Japanese harbors.

July Fourth of 1851 was a glorious day when Millard lay the cornerstone of the Capitol building. An expansion was due because of the growing number of states. He was also responsible for the iconic symmetrical design of the Capitol.[101]

In late 1851, we twice honored General Louis Kossuth, the Hungarian revolutionary, soldier, and patriot, with huge White House receptions. Invited were committees of the House and Senate, President of the Senate, and Speaker of the House. It was a delicate foreign relations issue, because Kossuth came seeking U.S. support for his own revolution. Kossuth pleaded that Hungarians were following "that principle upon which stands so gloriously the very political existence of the United States." But Millard was not interested in involving U.S. forces in European entanglements; he followed George Washington's policy of non-interference in European affairs.

Our greatest new luxury in the presidency was provided by the proud friends and admirers from Albany and New York. It was a splendid Clarence-style coach, with a body of lacquered green with an extravagant silver-mounted harness for my carriage horses. The door panels boasted the NYS Coat of arms with "Excelsior" painted on one. Its handles were mother-of-pearl with a silver lamp on each side. The seats and ten curtains were

---

[100] MF letter of 2/1852

[101] Caroline's scrapbook

Political Pitfalls of 1850

covered with blue watered silk texture.[102] All of the Fillmores rode grandly through the capital city in this splendid (though used) coach behind a liveried coachman.[103] Somehow a used coach for a "used presidency" seemed appropriate.

Kossuth's flattering gift of multi-lingual calligraphy--From the collection of the Aurora Historical Society

---

[102] Gleason's, May 10, 1851, following photo also

[103] Millard Fillmore Papers, Vol. XI, p. 304

Chapter Seven

LIVING IN THE WHITE HOUSE

My impressive husband certainly looked the part of president. He was declared by Horace Binney (who had known all the presidents from Washington to Grant) to be the most handsome president since Washington. He had that physical, manly beauty, accompanied by marked simplicity.[104]

When Millard entered the White House, he found it entirely destitute of books. I was in the habit of spending my leisure hours reading, almost studying. I was accustomed to being surrounded with books of reference, maps, and all the other acquirements of a well-furnished library; I found it difficult to content myself in a house devoid of such attractions. To meet this want, my husband asked of Congress and received an appropriation of $2000.[105]

From the collection of the Aurora Historical Society

My children and I did not arrive at the White House until October of 1850; I had needed to arrange for the care of my invalid sister Mary.[106] My first campaign on arriving was to join my husband in establishing a White

---

[104] Caroline's scrapbook

[105] Harriet Haven in "*The Ladies of the White House—1789-1881*"

[106] Snyder, *The Lady and the President*

House library—eleven presidents before us with not so much as a Bible. Previous presidents had brought and then removed their own libraries. I began my campaign soon after arriving by entertaining the most powerful Congressmen. I hosted a series of Thursday night dinner parties in the Congressional dining room until they agreed with my vision. At last, by March 3rd of 1851, the new congress permitted me to spend $250 "for the purchase of books for the library at the Executive Mansion...under the direction of the President of the U.S."[107]

They could have trusted me. I met with literary experts, and carefully chose <u>Vanity Fair</u> by Thackeray, *The Great Stone Face* and *The Scarlet Letter* by the profound Nathaniel Hawthorne, Emerson's brilliant essays, essays of Francis Bacon, Conversations with Lord Byron, *The Outlines of English Grammar*, and Webster's *Dictionary of the English Language*. I also included some Shakespeare, Milton and the best American and British poets. Also on my list were Burns, Irving, Sparks, Prescott, Jefferson, Dr. Johnson, Burke, Goldsmith, Calhoun, Clay and Webster. As fans of Sir Walter Scott, we were happy to obtain a complete set of his works, as well as his biography by John Gibson Lockhart. I also selected De Tocqueville's *Democracy in America, The Signers of the Declaration, The Federalist Papers, Aesop's Fables, Arabian Nights, Catlin's Indians of North America,* and *Bancroft's History of the United States.* Periodicals such as "The Whig and Democratic Review" and "The Niles Register" were included. Powers served as private secretary to his father and as the "Disbursing Agent for the purchase of books for the Executive Mansion's library."[108] Our selections were very diverse, covering history, science, literature, reference works, art, and the classics of the day.[109]

Entertaining was a big part of the job. My cousin, Dr. Cyrus Powers, a frequent visitor to the White House during our tenure, wrote to me in 1850… "I scarcely know whether to offer you congratulations or condolences. The 'honor' part is all well enough, but the idea of keeping open house for the

---

[107] Ibid

[108] Scarry

[109] Scarry

universe and being constantly prepared to 'receive' the world… like a sentinel always on guard, can hardly be so very pleasant. I think if I were a lady, and my husband should become president, I should run away."[110]

In gratitude to the men who had quickly stepped forward to form the president's Cabinet, I hosted a dinner on Thursday evening, October 11th, with Daniel Webster, Thomas Corwin, Mrs. A.H.H. Stuart, Nathan Hall and his wife, Senator James Pearce and more. Anna Brooks was a guest of mine who enjoyed singing, "In the Desert a Fountain is Springing," and Stephen Foster's "The Old Folks at Home." She was accompanied by Mrs. Brooks on the harp and by Abby on the piano.[111] A wood fire crackled at the hearth.

I set aside the most cheerful and largest room for my library on the second floor above the oval Blue Parlor. It was a non-descript room with a tobacco-defiled matting on the floor. The removal of the matting disclosed a Brussels carpet of wonderful design over which baskets too frail for their burden scattered roses of enormous size. I borrowed furniture from other rooms and

From the collection of the Aurora Historical Society

---

[110] Cyrus Powers to AF, Sept. 29, 1850. FPO

[111] MF to Dix, March 12, 1852

brought in some of my own favorite books. Around the oval-curved walls, we placed three- and five-tiered mahogany bookcases, adding Victorian couches and chairs. Abby's square rosewood piano, as well as her harp and guitar, were placed to make this our family's favorite room. It was here that the Fillmores invited our closest personal friends for happy musicals and informal visits. Even conscientious Millard usually succeeded in leaving his Executive Chamber by 10:30 at night to spend a pleasant hour in the library with the family.[112]

A properly "finished" graduate of Mrs. Sedgwick's school, 18-year-old Abby happily played and sang duets with me. Even shy Powers would sometimes join in singing Stephen Foster's latest tunes. Here Abby could practice her skills in painting or language, speaking French with ease and elegance, as well as Italian and some German.[113]

Unfortunately, I suffered with my permanently broken ankle, which made it hard to stand in line for two hours for Friday night levees. I used a liniment, wore silk, used oil of Origanian, crutches…for two years I suffered from pain and inflammation…never got better.[114] I would stay in bed all day to prepare for the ordeal, so my wonderful Abby helped a great deal. She served as unofficial White House hostess when I was unable to do so. Her musical talent was of a high order; she spoke French fluently, and her attractive personality and her rare conversational abilities won the admiration of the numerous guests to whom she was always ready to adapt herself.[115] Full of information and spirit, more anxious always to listen than to talk, yet never at a loss for something pleasant and entertaining to say, her countenance beamed with honesty and intellect. Her sweet cordial manners invited both confidence and respect.

On New Year's Eve of 1850, we welcomed crowds in the East Room. Abby joined Millard and me in greeting in the Blue Room. Young Abby

---

[112] Mrs. Solomon Haven, "Recollections of President Fillmore," Millard Fillmore Papers, Vol. XI, p. 492

[113] Ibid

[114] C.F. Perkins to AF, March 13, 1845, FPO

[115] Haven

was the talk of Washington, so self-possessed was she, with a rare ability to adapt her conversations to such a variety of guests with her fascinating stories. She was also uncommonly familiar with English literature. At one dinner party, Secretary of State Everett drew Abby's number as a dinner partner and described her as "a pretty, modest, unaffected girl of about 20, as much at ease at the head of the presidential tables as if she had been born a princess."[116]

Her friend Miss Miller from Buffalo visited and wrote, "After dinner we usually went upstairs to the library over the Blue Room with its wood fire. There was reading aloud, interesting conversation and always Miss Fillmore's charming music. Sometimes Powers would join his sister in singing."

The three Fillmore pianos were tuned nine times in one year.[117]

The new piano, bought for the White House on March 22, 1852, from William Hall & Son,[118] was a rosewood seven-octave square pianoforte. The public was keenly interested in all these developments, since the First Lady before me, Margaret Taylor, had been unhappy in the White House, spending her whole time knitting up in her room.

In January of 1852, Abby's suitor Hiram Day, a former law student of Millard's in Buffalo, visited Washington and stayed until March. Millard had the young couple invited to both Daniel Webster's ball and Mrs. Hall's ball, along with Powers

Mary Abigail—"Abby"
From the collection of the Aurora Historical Society

---

[116] Everett letter, Feb. 28, 1853

[117] Kirk, Elise, *Musical Highlights from the White House*, p. 70-71

[118] The Millard Fillmore Presidential Site's rosewood piano is from J. Sage & Sons.

and another young lady. The foursome traveled in the elegant family carriage and had the time of their lives. Millard treated Hiram like family, included him in family meals and, as Webster had done for him as a young congressman, had Day admitted to be able to argue before the Supreme Court.

We held Friday night levees from 8 to 10 and official dinners on Thursdays and Saturdays. Powers was his father's private secretary; it was his task to arrange all the details of these dinners, as well as Tuesday luncheons, including their entertainments. Band music was the usual fare, but no dancing. Sarah Polk, the fundamentalist wife of James Polk, had five years earlier banned card-playing and dancing at the White House; the Fillmores thought it prudent not to rock that boat. It was unusual to have alcohol served, but not forbidden. My husband rarely drank any alcohol, feeling he needed no artificial stimulants.[119]

A typical dinner began with mock turtle soup, and fish with butter sauce; a choice of nine entrees followed. Examples included "larded sweet breads with mushrooms, ham with macaroni, young ducks with brown sauce, fricassee of chicken, lamb cutlet with green peas, young pigeons with olives, croquet of chicken, fillet of veal with spinach, and roast chicken with salad." Dinners ended with as many as four desserts—Charlotte russe, blancmange, Madeira jelly, and vanilla ice cream—followed with fruits, coffee, and liqueurs. This was all served by six waiters in white gloves.[120]

Our White House had a staff of twelve—steward, doorkeeper, housekeeper, chambermaid, laundress, messenger, cook, coachman, waiter, fireman, hall maid, and washerwoman—for about $5000 a year.[121] The old Negro cook who had served many years at the White House was greatly upset when a woodstove of small-hotel-size was brought to his quarters. He had managed to prepare a fine State dinner for 36 people every Thursday in a huge fireplace, with cranes, hooks, pots, pans, kettles, and skillets; but

---

[119] *The Ladies of the White House*
[120] Severance, p. 515-516
[121] Scarry

he could not manage the drafts of the range. It ended in a journey of the President to the Patent Office to inspect the model and restore peace to the kitchen. Contrary to popular legend, Millard did NOT put the first bathtub in the White House, but he did install the first wood cookstove.

From the collection of the Smithsonian, Abigail's lavender gown (not inaugural)

In February of 1851, I suffered the loss of my dear sister Mary, aged 55. Also, I was still in mourning for the passing of my last brother, David, in 1850; I wore almost exclusively black, and for fancy occasions, the semi-mourning color of lavender. (Incidentally, I was the first lady of the White House to wear a dress stitched with the newly invented sewing machine.)[122]

In May of 1851, we visited Buffalo for the first time since Millard had become president. The occasion was the opening of the Erie Railway from New York to Dunkirk. Webster, Hall, Crittenden, Stephen Douglas, and many more dignitaries joined us. After the rail ride, we took the side-wheel steamer *Mayflower* from Dunkirk to Buffalo. The harbor was decorated with bunting; the wharves were thronged with cheering citizens. At the foot of Main Street, we entered carriages, driving up through a tunnel of flags. The sidewalks, windows and roofs were full of admirers, fluttering handkerchiefs and ringing cheers. As the procession passed the corner of Swan Street where an immense banner announced, "Welcome Home," a troop of young girls stepped out and strewed flowers into and under the carriage. Millard was so moved.[123]

In mid-June of 1851, our whole family and Mrs. Leland (my niece from

---

[122] Smithsonian exhibit of First Lady gowns

[123] Caroline's scrapbook

Wisconsin), traveled to Auburn for a few hours. We also went south in Cayuga County to visit friends and relatives in Kelloggsville and Moravia.[124]

Abigail Fillmore, from the collection of the Aurora Historical Society

The summers in the White House were hardly healthy. The mosquitoes of the Potomac River were feared to carry malaria; the White House walls were damp. So Abby and I escaped, summering at the ocean at Newport. Millard joined us with great fanfare on September 16th, leaving for festivities in Boston and returning on the 19th. Alas, I reinjured my ankle in a fall during our Newport vacation.[125]

When my father-in-law Nathaniel was eighty, he paid a visit to his son in the White House, the first father to be able to exercise that privilege. Our pastor, Rev. Hosmer, accompanied him, noting, "Was there ever such a contrast as Millard and his venerable father here and the baby in the sap trough?" Millard, born into complete poverty, had been placed in such a humble cradle.[126] Nathaniel was asked how a man should raise a son to be president. The old gentleman replied, "Teach him ever to speak the truth."[127] We held a State Banquet to honor him, introducing him with pride to all the dignitaries and ambassadors.

I did rock the boat by going about Washington freely to gather cultural experiences. Abby and I attended lectures, banquets, art exhibits, and literary meetings. Millard and I followed the social etiquette of Washington at that time by never accepting social invitations, but Abby happily represented us at many parties.

The most exciting concerts to attend in December of 1850 in the Na-

---

[124] *Daily Advertiser*, Auburn, June 19-23, 1851

[125] Severance, MF to Daniel Webster, Sept. 12, 1851

[126] Caroline's scrapbook

[127] Ibid

tional Theater were that of Jenny Lind, the "Swedish Nightingale," brought to America by promoter P.T. Barnum in 1850-51. She sang in 130 concerts in 24 cities, earning herself $187,500—the equivalent today of $7.6 million.[128] We could not have missed the event, so the whole Fillmore family and Cabinet attended. Miss Lind later visited the White House where I was able to interview her about her native Sweden. She wrote to a friend after our visit, "Such simplicity in this American court!" I hope that was a compliment.

Nathaniel Fillmore, 1851
Public domain, in the collection of the Buffalo History Museum

Cousin Cyrus commented that three-hour-long state dinners were held twice a week. "Tradition was that by invitation each member of the House, Senate, judges of the Supreme Court, cabinet members and their wives dined at least once during the winter, some several times. Other guests were high-ranking officers of the Army and Navy, visitors from all regions of the nation and distinguished foreigners."[129]

On November 19 of 1851, Dr. Powers described the President and our family standing together. The Cabinet ladies and guests of the House were in the second row, a little to one side where their acquaintances could speak to them without interrupting the procession. I wore wine-colored velvet with Honiton lace and a diamond brooch. Abby wore a silk of a changeable green and red, a pattern brocade with three flounces and fine French muslin embroideries in waist and sleeves.

---

[128] Rosenberg, Charles, *Jenny Lind in America*, p. 88
[129] Cyrus Powers letter, FPO

First came the Corps Diplomatique, the gentlemen in regular court dress, stiff with embroidery and gold lace. The ladies were dressed in the style of the winter, all very handsomely, of course. The President received in the Blue Room. Persons entered the Red Room and passed into the Blue, thence through the Green Drawing Room and into the great East Room from which there was an exit built from the windows. The Blue Room was full of these richly dressed men and women.[130]

Cousin Cyrus wrote, "I never saw a more united and loving family--admirable, able, pure and patriotic...his domestic life simply perfect."[131]

On December 21 of 1852, an acquaintance remarked, "the President's Mansion was open as usual and was filled by a stream of gay and brilliant visitors, who for three hours kept all its spacious salons crowded, tending to the Chief Magistrate of the Nation the greetings and compliments of the season."[132]

I had been having some trouble with my eyesight and had seen Dr. Joseph Turnbull, a London eye specialist, for help. One evening, a friend brought a New Orleans novelist, Miss Helen DeKroyft, to my library. Miss DeKroyft had been blind for seven years and asked me to introduce her to Dr. Turnbull for a cure. I honored her request, and in my last month in the White House, the doctor performed an unusual operation on the novelist that restored her sight. She wrote me a wonderful thank you:

> "Dear, dear Mrs. Fillmore,
> I shall see again! Oh, I shall see again! After seven years a prisoner to darkness. Oh, how shall I ever find words to thank you for sending me to him! Never, never shall I look on the flowers, or the white snows of winter, or the blue sky, but I shall remember to whom I owe it all.... You have made my heart glad, and now at last, you have turned my dark eyes toward the light. I thank you, I bless you, I love you, and always, I shall pray for you.
> Your most humble, most devoted friend,
> S. Helen DeKroyft"

---

[130] Hollingsworth, p. 312-313

[131] Cyrus Powers letter

[132] Singleton, p. 19

Little did Helen know how much I would need her prayers once our time in the White House had come to an end.

Chapter Eight

A SAD RETURN TO BUFFALO

Our farewells to this memorable period of our lives began on Sunday, January 23 of 1853. We enjoyed an excursion to Mount Vernon with Washington Irving and some of our family after breakfast at the White House.[133]

From the collection of Aurora Historical Society

On February 28, we held the concluding presidential reception, enjoying a hearty acknowledgement of true esteem from thousands of visitors. The crowds basked in the array of beauty, fashion and brilliancy that abounded in the White House.[134]

As I confessed to my sister-in-law Julia, I was "eagerly looking forward to a return to my old home...."[135] But the Buffalo home had tenants. "We had fondly looked forward to the time when we should assemble our little family around our own domestic hearth and enjoy life as we had more years been permitted to enjoy it. I should be no more harassed with the cares of state, or worn down with professional labors, but spend my time in cheerful

---

[133] Singleton, p. 22

[134] Caroline's scrapbook

[135] Gen. James Grant Wilson, Jan. 7, 1878

amusements with my family. This seemed to be the consummation of our hopes and the end of all our arduous toils, and we often talked of it with great satisfaction."[136]

We packed papers, correspondence, a painting, harp, music stand, books, wines, glassware, and my special collection of shell craft in wooden boxes and trunks…to be conveyed by steamer to New York and Albany, then to Buffalo by Erie Canal.[137]

One of the last things Millard did when he left office was to sell the fancy silver harness and splendid coach, the welcoming gift from New Yorkers, too princely for our life in Buffalo. He spent the proceeds on a twelve-piece set of silver plates. They were made to order and the server had inscribed on it: "The carriage and horses generously presented to Mrs. Millard Fillmore by the citizens of New York in 1850; having been sold in 1853, the proceeds are invested in this set of plate as a perpetual memento of gratitude to the donor." The main server was inscribed, "intended to descend as an heirloom in the Fillmore family 'as an imperishable record of his gratitude.'"

The grand "used" carriage given to Abigail Fillmore, for a "used presidency"

---

[136] MF to Julia Harris, April 13, 1853

[137] MF letters, March 3, 1853

A Sad Return to Buffalo

As the transfer of power commenced, Millard greeted incoming President Franklin Pierce warmly, taking him to a lecture on English humorists by William Makepeace Thackeray. They then toured on the Potomac on the *Vixen*. We also hosted a White House dinner and public reception for Pierce, Thackeray, and Washington Irving.

We attended Franklin Pierce's inauguration on March 4th of 1853; I was the first first lady of the White House to attend my husband's successor's inauguration. There I stood with my literary friends William Makepeace Thackeray and Washington Irving in the raw northeasterly wind and whipping snow. I returned chilled to the Willard Hotel. Millard, ever the gracious gentleman, in the absence of Mrs. Pierce, helped the new president receive at the White House after the inauguration ceremonies.

On Sunday, March 6th, I attended church, appearing in good health. In the afternoon we rode to Georgetown to visit Millard's sister Olive and his brothers Calvin and Cyrus, who had been staying in the White House before the inauguration. Every boarding house and hotel was full. That evening, I became ill with a severe cold and high fever.

On Monday morning I shopped with Abby. Millard and I had made happy plans to build a new house in Buffalo. We planned to travel home by way of touring the South—through Virginia, North Carolina, South Carolina, Georgia, Alabama, New Orleans, Mississippi, Tennessee, Kentucky, Arkansas, Missouri, Illinois, Wisconsin, and Michigan, arriving at home by May 1st.[138] Neither of us had ever been south of Richmond, so we were looking forward to a great adventure.

But suddenly on Wednesday morning, I woke up very ill. A physician was called. Millard cancelled a dinner at the White House with President Pierce. I had difficulty breathing, talking, even lying down. The only way I could sleep was with my head on a table to clear my congestion. Dear Millard read to me a great deal, hoping to distract me from my affliction. He wrote to his sister Julia after the first week of my illness that I spoke very little. He wrote to the new President Pierce that I was indeed very sick

---

[138] Caroline's scrapbook

and that I was remembering that premonition of not seeing many more birthdays. The cold progressed to pneumonia. Two nurses and four different physicians were in attendance. Millard, Abby and Powers were at my bedside.

By Tuesday, March 29, I worsened. Told by the physicians that I might not live beyond an hour, Millard wrote, "it almost unmanned me."[139]

I now transfer my voice to my faithful son and firstborn, Millard Powers Fillmore.

At 9 a.m. on Wednesday, March 30 of 1853, my dear mother died. Pierce closed all public offices. The Senate adjourned.

Did the White House have a curse attached to it? A Buffalo paper opined, "General Jackson's wife, General Harrison, President Tyler's wife and General Taylor all were summoned to the tomb while inmates of the presidential mansion. President Polk survived his residence at the White House just a short time, Mrs. Fillmore still shorter."[140]

Just two months earlier, the new President Pierce had lost his only remaining son, eleven-year-old Benjamin, in a train-derailment in New England, right in front of his parents' eyes. Benjamin's two little brothers had also died, one at birth and one of typhus at the age of four. Mrs. Pierce collapsed in grief and would spend most of her White House tenure in mourning. So much tragedy!

Father wrote to his brother Charles, "My beloved wife is no more…Her disease was inflammation on the lungs arising from a severe cold, taken about the 6th of March, which soon terminated in a dropsy of the lungs. She bore all her sufferings with uncomplaining fortitude, and at last expired without a struggle or a groan."[141]

Father said after her death, "For 27 years, my entire married life, I was always greeted with a happy smile."[142]

---

[139] MF to Julia Harris, April 13, 1853

[140] *Buffalo Commercial Advertiser & Journal*, April 4, 1853

[141] MF to Chas. Fillmore, April 5, 1853, from Buffalo

[142] MF to Julia Harris, April 13, 1853

A Sad Return to Buffalo

The very next morning at 6 a.m., Father, Abby, and I left Washington, DC. In a private train car, we sat beside her coffin. On April 1st, we arrived in Buffalo. After a brief funeral ceremony on Saturday, April 2nd, Mother was laid to rest in Forest Lawn Cemetery. Abby stayed with Mrs. Haven, I went to my grandfather's home in East Aurora, and Father stayed with Nathan Hall until our home could again be available.

Washington Irving felt guilty, I'm afraid. He wrote, "I almost think poor Mrs. Fillmore must have received her death warrant while standing by my side on the marble terrace of the Capitol, exposed to the chilly wind and snow, listening to the inaugural speech of her husband's successor."

Mother's obituary was deservedly glowing—"inquiring, amiable, sensible, Fillmore's truest friend, counselor, his right arm. She was an accomplished woman and musician, having excellent refined manners, sense, grace, dignity, habits, and studious industry. She sought to make those about her happy and to make her home the seat of intellectual pursuit. She loved books, flowers, and the French and German languages."

Father wrote to social reformer and friend, Dorothea Dix—"...it does not seem like home. The light of the house is gone; and I can never hope to enjoy life again as I have heretofore."[143]

To his sister, he noted, "...she has trained my dear, ever dearly dear children in wisdom and virtue, and they are also spared to comfort and bless me. Yet my nights are solitary, and my house is desolate."[144]

Lloyd Slade wrote to Father about Mother: "The early strong and abiding love for you which I have often witnessed... used to meet her gentle and heartfelt embrace. She had a liberal and fruitful mind."[145] Aunt Julia Harris wrote of her brother, "He would kneel before his wife to adjust her overshoes on the way to their carriage. Always courteous and attentive to her."[146]

---

[143] MF to DD, May 22, 1853

[144] MF to Julia Harris, April 13, 1853

[145] Slade to MF, June 22, 1860, FPO

[146] Severance, Mrs. A. Harris to MF, Feb. 5, 1860, FPO

We received the news that the fleet Father sent to Japan arrived in July of 1853, frightening the Japanese with their smoke-belching ships. The Americans sat in the harbor for eight days, waiting for a response to Perry's letter which had been elegantly sent in a rosewood box. Finally, the answer came, wrapped in velvet and placed in a sandalwood box. Perry came ashore with two bands playing "Hail, Columbia." What really surprised the Japanese were the two Negro bodyguards Perry brought, as well as blondes, redheads and brunettes. The wary Japanese and Americans met in a canvas tent. A red cloth floor hid ten samurai, who were ready to hop out and attack the foreigners if necessary.[147]

The nine-day visit went well. Perry departed, returning the next February loaded with gifts. This time five hundred American sailors went ashore in 27 boats, while three ships' bands played "The Star-Spangled Banner." Perry delivered lavish gifts, as did the Japanese. They signed the treaty, allowing access for the Americans to two small ports. This was the end of the Japanese isolation, and the entry of Japan into the modern world. It is such a point of pride that Father initiated this world-changing exchange.

Square piano and bound music books of Abby Fillmore, in the collection of the Aurora Historical Society

The rumors of Father remarrying appeared quickly. In February of 1854, a published report appeared in a Washington paper that he would marry 32-year-old Miss Elizabeth Porter of Niagara Falls, the only daughter of the late General Peter Porter, hero of the War of 1812. A reigning belle in Western New York, she carried with her the vast Porter estate, including Goat Island and other lucrative property in Niagara Falls.[148]

---

[147] Rhoda Blumberg, *Commodore Perry in the Land of the Shogun*, (Lothrop, Lee & Shepherd, 1985)
[148] Caroline's scrapbook

A Sad Return to Buffalo

This rumor proved to be pure folly.

In Mother's absence, Abby did her best to fill in, caring for both Father and me. By her entire devotion to the duties of keeping house, she relieved Father from all household cares, and displayed those high domestic and social qualities which gave a grace and charm, as well as system and regularity to the home over which she presided. Her whole heart and mind were given to promote our father's happiness and that of mine as well. We repaid her devotion with the kindest and most grateful affection.

In June Father took Abby, Nathan Hall, and me along for "the greatest railroad Excursion of the Age," a ride on the new Chicago and Rock Island line. In mid-July, the vivacious Abby tempted fate at a fun-filled party of 23 friends, picnicking at Rock City, a playground of giant boulders near Olean, New York. She laughed all day and sang "Hail, Columbia" as the group emerged from the woods—the life of the party.[149] Her friend Susan Johnson hosted the crowd at her Ellicottville home for dinner on that evening. Abby arrived late and was to be the thirteenth person to sit at the table. Susan quickly rose as Abby sat to keep her precious friend from bringing herself bad luck. But Abby just laughed at her and raising her glass of wine, said, "I drink to the discouragement of all superstition."[150] Before leaving, she made plans to see her friends the next week to visit the mighty Niagara Falls.

The next Tuesday, July 25th of 1854, Abby and her friend took a 2 p.m. German lesson in Buffalo. Abby then announced her intention to visit Grandfather Nate in East Aurora. She wanted to help our grandparents settle in their new house. Protective Father was not enthusiastic about Abby taking the stagecoach alone. I volunteered to drive her, but she refused and took a carriage by herself, knowing that there would be no room for both of us to spend the night.

She spent the evening happily helping old Nathaniel and Eunice to make this house their own. But suddenly, dreaded cholera struck her, ironically, on its last epidemic pass through Western New York. She went to bed at

---

[149] Buffalo Daily, 8/4/54

[150] Susan wrote this on the back of Abby's letter, Library of Congress, found by the author.

9 and became sick but didn't want to disturb her grandparents. Finally at midnight she called out for them in fear for her life. We were summoned from Buffalo, as was the doctor from next door, but before Father and I could reach East Aurora, beautiful Abby was unconscious. By 11 a.m., she was gone.[151]

The next day, she was interred next to Mother in Forest Lawn.[152]

At age 22, Abby was in her prime; her loss hit both Father and me very, very hard, only sixteen months after Mother's death. My dear sister was a lady of many excellencies and much promise. Not only was she beautiful, but her intellect was improved by substantial culture. Her manner was quiet and retiring, but her character was natural and independent. Universally beloved in Buffalo, she survived the trying ordeal of hostessing at the White House, commanding admiration and respect, displaying at all times frankness, sincerity, discretion and good sense. Basking in the sunshine of rank and fortune and fashion, with all the glare of Washington society, she retained her native simplicity.[153]

Harp and music stand, gifts of Hiram Day, in the collection of the Aurora Historical Society

My sister never saw or read of a kind or noble deed that her eyes did not fill with tears. She clung to her old friends without regard to their position

---

[151] *Buffalo Commercial Advertiser*, July 28, 1854

[152] Ibid

[153] Caroline's scrapbook

in life and her time and talents seemed devoted to their happiness. She was thinking constantly of some little surprise, some gift, some journey, some pleasure, by which she could contribute to the enjoyment of others.

Abby was said to have almost masculine judgment and the most feminine tenderness. With a keen sense of the ridiculous, overflowing with vivacious wit and humor, all her views of life were nevertheless grave and serious. Her sense of duty led her to cultivate all her talents; she was one of the most accomplished young women anyone knew. Her advantages had been great, and she had reaped their entire fruit. Familiar with English literature, she also spoke French with ease and elegance, was well-versed in Italian and had recently made great progress in her German studies. She could draw and was just starting to study sculpture, but it was music that gave her great pleasure, both on the harp and the piano.[154] Hiram Day, who had gifted Abby a beautiful harp and music stand, lived to be an old man and never married.

As for me, the light of the whole world had died with Abby and Mother. I never enjoyed life from that time forth.[155]

---

[154] Caroline's scrapbook

[155] Memorial Meeting of the Erie County Bar Asso., 1890

Chapter Nine

FORGETTING OUR TROUBLES

Although my father did not believe it proper to practice law as a former president, I resumed my successful law practice, this time in partnership with E. Carlton Sprague. But I chose not to be a trial lawyer. My timidity precluded that sort of thing. Perhaps my introversion was based on my family tragedies. This was a gloom from which I never recovered. I also felt deeply the criticism of my dear Father for his service to the country. There were those in Buffalo who were openly critical of his part in the Compromise of 1850.

Almost immediately after Abby's funeral, Father and I sought out the comfort of friends and relatives in Moravia, Skaneateles, Montville, and New Hope. Dorothea Dix wrote with a prescription for Millard's depression—a trip to Europe to "occupy the winter in seeing what is most worthy of study and observation in the old civilized world."[156]

He departed for Europe in the spring of 1855 with various members of his presidential cabinet, and Buffalo friends, E. R. Jewett and Dr. Thomas Foote. The voyage on

Queen Victoria, Wikipedia

---
[156] Snyder, p. 212

the steamer *Atlantic* was far from perfect. His companion, General James Wilson, said that for a day and a half, "we were in a terrible storm which swept our decks, destroying three boats, one of the wheelhouses, and severely injuring several of the sailors. To add to the terror of the situation, we were surrounded by icebergs. Many of the passengers gave themselves up for lost, and I shall never forget the tone and look of Mr. Fillmore as he said, while the storm was at its worst, 'I wish I were at home. If I ever reach Buffalo, I shall remain there.'"[157]

Father was invited to visit Queen Victoria, but was initially hesitant because he was unwilling to appear in court dress. When the regent heard this, she sent a message that he should wear whatever he pleased.[158] But when he dined at Buckingham Palace, he was required to wear the cocked hat, knee breeches and sword of the court costume. Her Majesty admired his graceful and dignified bearing and address as superior to any other American she had met.[159]

On his return from the royal event, he laughed merrily to his friends, "Well, gentlemen, I never expected to come to this!"[160]

Oxford University offered to bestow Father with the Degree of Classical Languages, but Millard humbly declined, feeling the honor was offered more because he was a former president than for his own intellect. "I had not the advantage of a classical education, and no man should in my opinion accept a degree that he cannot read."[161]

Perhaps he remembered the mockery Andrew Jackson had made of an honorary degree from Harvard in 1833. Jackson ended his speech with all the Latin he knew: "E pluribus unum! Sine qua non! Multum in parvo! Quid pro quo! Ne plus ultra!" (this translated means, "United we stand, without any means, great in little, something given for something else, none better.")

---

[157] Gen. Wilson
[158] Caroline's scrapbook
[159] Caroline's scrapbook
[160] Ibid
[161] Gen. Wilson

They toured through Germany, returning to Paris for the International Exposition by October. While in Paris, Father met with Emperor Louis Napoleon.[162]

The three Buffalonians traveled to Brussels, Cologne, then boated up the Rhine to Geneva, Switzerland. There was hardly a city missed—Munich, Vienna, Prague, Dresden, Berlin, Hamburg, Bremen, Dusseldorf, Amsterdam, Antwerp, Florence, Rome, and Naples. Father's affliction with inflamed eyes prevented their intended tour of the Holy Land.[163]

After much controversy, Father did meet with Pope Pius IX, serving from 1846 to 1878--the longest serving Pope in history. From what I heard, everyone thought they looked alike!

Since Father had joined the new American Party, derisively known as the "Know Nothing Party," he had realized that meeting with this head of the Catholic world could be a dilemma. His alliance with this party was a puzzle to me; it was in many ways the opposite of his original party affiliation with the Anti-Masonics. To join the American Party, one had to follow an elaborate secret ritual and unite with the Order of the Star-Spangled Banner, an anti-Catholic secret society. Only native-born, white Americans with no Catholic connections were eligible.[164]

The members of the American Party feared the huge influx of immigrants, who were now arriving at a rate three times faster than ever before in the nineteenth century. The Know-Nothings wanted to make it impossible for these "invaders" to hold public office in the United States.

Father wrote home: "My opportunity of comparing my own country and the condition of our peoples with those of Europe has only served to increase my admiration and love of our blessed land of liberty, and I shall return to it without even a desire ever to cross the Atlantic again."[165]

While still in Rome in February of 1856, Father received a letter telling him that he had been nominated as the American Party's presidential can-

---

[162] Ibid

[163] Caroline's scrapbook

[164] Lawrence, p. 330

[165] *Mr. Fillmore at Home: His Reception at NY & Brooklyn*, 1856

didate. Friends wrote, begging him to run again. In May, he wrote back that he would accept the nomination and run for the presidency that fall. I feel he accepted this nomination because he, and others, believed he was the only one who could keep the country together. The Republican Party was too aligned with the abolitionists, the Democrats were pro-slavery, and the Whig Party had disintegrated. Father disliked the Republicans, predicting that if this extremist group ever elected a president, the South would surely secede.

Campaign poster from 1856 from the collection of the Aurora Historical Society

Finally, Father returned to the United States, arriving in New York harbor in June. The ship he was on fired its guns and rockets until it was docked. The wharf answered with a fifty-gun salute from the New Jersey shore. Over two thousand people waited to greet my father, now the presidential candidate. They paraded up Canal to Broadway. From almost every window, ladies waved white handkerchiefs in greeting.

On the whistle-stop train ride home, Father greeted cheering crowds in city after city, spreading the message that Americans should govern Americans. Fillmore said, "I regret to say that men who come from the monarchies of the Old World are prepared neither by education, habits of thought, or knowledge of our institutions to govern Americans."[166]

At long last in Buffalo, he had the sweetest welcome of all at Niagara Square. Thirteen beautiful young girls paraded up to him, dressed in white muslin and blue silk gowns with blue silk ribbons in their braided hair. Each held a bouquet of flowers in one hand and the American flag in the other, presenting them all to Fillmore, who returned the gifts with a handshake and a warm smile. The last girl was a beautiful little innocent of four years; Father took her in his arms, giving her a kiss. Greeting the crowd, he said, "My mind has often teemed with yearnings to my home in Western New York; and I have longed for the opportunity of once more beholding this beautiful Queen City of the Empire State, and of breathing again the fresh air that blows from her lakes."

When he finally closed the door on our home on Franklin, a band outside played, "Home, Sweet Home."[167]

The Republicans had chosen John Fremont as their candidate. He was famous as a pathfinder, having made exploratory trips to the West with Kit Carson. On one such trip, he supposedly discovered the "woolly horse," equal parts of elephant, deer, buffalo, camel, sheep, and horse. Naturally, such a creature belonged with the famous circus-man P.T. Barnum. In derision, the Democrats and Know-Nothings called Fremont and all Republicans the "Woollies."

---

[166] W. L. Barre, *The Life and Public Services of Millard Fillmore*, p. 241
[167] Severance

Edward Bates, a former Whig, and later Lincoln's attorney general, opined, "Nothing but Fillmore's election..." could fix the state of the national divisions. "And my prayer to God is that He will bless the nation by enabling us to place at its head a man of moderation, order and peace."[168]

By November, the votes were cast, and Father came in third with 22% of the popular vote. In the Electoral College, he had only Maryland's vote, though three other states were only 2% short of giving their electoral votes to him. He was humiliated. Democrat Buchanan was the winner with only 45% of the popular vote, the first unmarried president elected.

After the campaign, Father was a gracious loser. "I envy not my successful rivals, but sincerely hope that the one [James Buchanan] on whom the people have conferred the highest honors of the Republic, may so discharge the responsible duties of his exalted station as to restore peace and harmony to the conflicting sections, and maintain the honor and glory of the nation. If this be done, I can cheerfully forgive all my enemies for the falsehoods which they may have published against me, by misrepresenting my sentiments, both North and South.[169]

Being a well-known and eligible bachelor, Father drew continued speculation about searching for a new partner. There were rumors that he had admired a Catholic lady from Montreal, even attending a mass in that city.[170] Again, no truth to it. But soon there was some genuine activity on the prospects of a wealthy Albany widow.

---

[168] Bates letter to MF, 9/24/56

[169] Caroline's scrapbook

[170] Ibid

CAROLINE'S ROOTS & SECOND MARRIAGES

Caroline Carmichael, daughter of Charles Carmichael and Temperance Blachley Carmichael, was born in Morristown, NJ, on October 21 of 1813. Charles was a blueblood, a descendant of 1640 Pilgrim John Odgen. Sadly, Caroline was orphaned at age 11; her mother died in 1818 and father in 1824. She was moved into the Schuyler Mansion in Albany with her Uncle John Bryan, a successful furrier who lived in the mansion from 1818 to 1848.

Built in 1761, the Schuyler Mansion was one of the finest examples of Georgian architecture in America. This majestic home had hosted George Washington, Benjamin Franklin, and John Jay. Alexander Hamilton and Elizabeth Schuyler were married there in 1780.

Caroline Fillmore--From the collection of the Aurora Historical Society

In November of 1832 at age 19, Caroline married Ezekiel C. McIntosh, a widower whose first wife had died the previous year. McIntosh lived from 1806 to May of 1855. He was a prosperous Troy crockery merchant, a founder of the University of Rochester, and president of the Albany Schenectady Railroad, which was part of the Mohawk and Hudson Railroad. When Uncle John Bryan was in danger of losing the mansion in 1846, Ezekiel bought it.

Watercolor drawing of the Schuyler Mansion made by Philip Hooker in 1818

McIntosh was in the opposite political camp from Fillmore, working unsuccessfully to defeat Fillmore's run for NYS Comptroller. Ironically, McIntosh was given $20,000 to fund Fillmore's defeat, but the money was never used for that purpose; Caroline carried that into her next marriage.

In 1853 and 1854, Caroline loved touring western Europe, Turkey, Greece, and Egypt with Mrs. Henry Rathbone and Miss Helen Shirtliff. When Ezekiel died at age 49 in 1855, Caroline was only 42. They had just completed their last tour of Europe together. Her husband had left her $20,000 in securities and the use of the mansion during her lifetime; the whole of his estate was worth $100,000 [2024 equivalent of $3.5 million.] His last wish was "that every member of the family show the greatest kindness to my beloved wife, an orphan. Indeed, she needs every kindness and attention."[171]

---

[171] Ginny Bowers, researcher for Schuyler mansion

Caroline's Roots & Second Marriages

My father, now 57, met Caroline, who was at that time a 42-year-old wealthy childless widow, at an Albany party on March of 1857, given by Mrs. Ira Harris. Her late husband had been a state assemblyman with Father and was currently the executor of the McIntosh will. To quote Mrs. Harris, Caroline was "…not the least interesting part of the whole setting, a very bright little body, with unfailing resources in her own cheerful temperament and cultivated mind. But despite all this, she finds herself very lonely at times, alone in that great house."[172]

By July (a mere four months after meeting), Caroline and my father were discussing where to live when married—Buffalo or Albany. Her judgment and inclinations were at war… "I am not shackled to this spot as to prefer freedom of solitude to you. To teach me to subdue, renounce my love, my life, myself to you…My only object is to find the means most likely to contribute to your happiness without interfering with those you love. Neither do I consider, I am leaving a certainty for an uncertainty to go with you, if you really can give me your love and affection; but if you cannot do this entirely, I may despair. Let me know it now."[173]

They agreed on a rare pre-nuptial agreement; Caroline held her money and property in her own name. She made Father the manager of her estate at a $10,000 annual salary, requiring a strict accounting for every dollar he spent from her capital.

Father commissioned a portrait of Caroline by artist Miss Wagner of Albany in 1857.[174]

But there are no love letters between them—they were either destroyed or she didn't save them. Father wrote to his dear friend Dorothea Dix, "Pray come and see how contented and happy we are."[175]

The new Fillmore couple bought the Hollister mansion--the biggest, gaudiest Gothic mansion in Buffalo (52 Niagara Square), for $15,900 [in 2024 dollars, $560,000]. They remained at the Schuyler Mansion until the

---

[172] Snyder, President and the Lady, p. 278

[173] CF to MF, July 25, 1857, FPO

[174] Caroline's first will

[175] MF to Dix, May 17, 1858

Buffalo mansion renovations were complete. The Schuyler mansion was then rented to wealthy Irish businessman John Tracey.

From the postcard collection of the author

Father married Caroline, in white silk with a lace veil, on Feb. 10, 1858. For the second time, she married a widower in the "Hamilton Room" of the Schuyler Mansion in Albany, NY—Father was 58, she 45. The ceremony was performed by her Baptist minister, Rev. Dr. William Hague. Following the vows, the wedding party was treated to an 11 PM performance by the band of the 76th regiment before the Fillmores retired to the groom's rooms at the Delavan House across town.[176]

---

[176] NYS History blog.org 10/10/2016

The *Utica Observer* reported that on their way to Buffalo, the new couple dined at Bagg's Hotel. Father was as attentive to his bride "as that charming lady could desire. Mrs. Fillmore is quite petite in figure, has a brilliant eye and winning face, is 'spirituelle' and accomplished, and is the possessor of a very handsome fortune."[177]

Finally, they moved into the Hollister House, now known as the Fillmore House. They shared it with me--the perennial bachelor. Months later after their winter-long honeymoon in Europe, they began what would be their sixteen-year marriage before Father's death. In the 1860s, Caroline's mental and physical health unfortunately declined while Millard enjoyed great health. She clearly enjoyed her status as the wife of a former president. An avid scrapbooker, Caroline clipped and saved hundreds of articles mentioning her famous husband.

Millard wrote again to his friend Dorothea about life in the Buffalo mansion. "Indeed, I think we are both more contented at home than abroad, and our summer climate, as you are aware, is most delightful in Buffalo. Many of our people, it is true, go away for a month or two, either from habit or fashion, to meet society at the watering places; but really, I do not think they find anywhere a more delightful summer or autumnal climate than this. And when business or a desire to visit friends does not call me away, I prefer to enjoy it. My own house is the most comfortable place I can find, and my wife and library, with the occasional friends who drop in, are the most charming society."[178]

On Father's first birthday after the wedding, he surprised Caroline in the library after breakfast with a pair of sable fur cuffs and a purse with $500 [in 2024 dollars, $14,000] in gold for "pin money." She wrote in her diary, "I do value these acts exceedingly as marks of affection and love. Though every want is supplied, still we like to be remembered by those we love."[179]

While in Paris, Father selected, as a surprise to Caroline, a set of nine cut steel ornaments—brooch, long pendant earrings, comb, oval belt hook,

---

[177] Caroline's scrapbook

[178] MF to Dix, Oct. 9, 1858

[179] Caroline's scrapbook

belt clasp, sleeve buttons, cap pins, cross-cut brilliant on velvet. He commissioned her portrait as well.

On Saturday, February 16th of 1861, President-elect Abraham Lincoln came through Buffalo on his way to his inauguration. The next day, Caroline and Father accompanied him to the First Unitarian Church. Father stood in his usual place, serene and courtly; next to him was the gaunt, melancholy Abe, with his head bent reverently in prayer.

They appeared together on the balcony of the American Hotel to greet a huge crowd. Together they attended a public meeting about several Western Indian tribes.[180]

Mural at the Buffalo History Museum

We did not forget East Aurora at this time. Father visited his Uncle Calvin at his large red frame house between the two villages. Calvin leased part of his home to shoemaker David Johnson, who kept his shoemaking business in the front room. Johnson cared for the old colonel in his own home until his death. Great-uncle Calvin was a character whose daily custom was to visit the village store, the tavern, the blacksmith shop, or the

---

[180] Rayback, p. 423.

cobbler shop to read Shakespeare to whomever cared to listen. Almost daily he drew a crowd because of his dramatic elocution.[181] He worked Shakespearean quotes into all his conversations.

One day in Johnson's shop, Father sat in an armchair, reading Shakespeare to his uncle and the cobbler. Eighty-three-year-old Calvin gave orders to the ex-president on what to read, "Read that portion of *Mac Beth*..." and "Now, Millard, read that passage with the soliloquy from *Hamlet*." Millard would graciously turn to the desired page and quote it for an hour or more. Tiptoeing in, a neighbor quietly seated himself and listened. All that could be heard besides the words of the Bard of Avon was the intermittent clatter of the cobbler's hammer. When Millard finally tired, he quietly passed the treasured volume to his uncle, shook everyone's hands and hurried off in time to catch the stagecoach back to Buffalo.[182] My esteemed Great-uncle Calvin died on October 22 of 1865 at the age of 90.

By this time, I was serving as Clerk of the US District Court for the Northern District of New York, appointed by Judge Nathan Hall. I remained there until Hall was replaced by Judge Wallace. I also served as a US Commissioner.

The Fillmore mansion was kind, delightful, pleasant, and hospitable,[183] a large, high-gabled Gothic Revival mansion of 20-some rooms. The windows had a pointed arch; two octagonal spires were on each side of the entrance. The top of each spire was ornamented with a pointed roof and a Gothic cross. A large turret tower was at the west end of

---

[181] *Times*, 10/27/1928

[182] Caroline's Scrapbook & *Times*, 10/27/1928

[183] Cyrus Power to MF, Jan. 22, 1857

the three-story building. It had a distinct gaudiness with its many peaked eaves, below which hung wooden brackets of intricate design; a long elaborate porch graced the front.[184]

The double front doors sometimes opened to two tiny Scotch terriers, bred by our butler, Jamieson.[185]

The family enjoyed a lovely rhythm of a few weeks in August at Saratoga at the Congress Hall, occasionally visiting Albany and New York City. But Caroline was fragile, spending weeks at a time in bed with fatigue and anxiety.[186]

Father's courtesy and attention to his wife were always marked, and some of us can remember more than once seeing him kneel before his wife and carefully adjusting her overshoes on their way to parties. He was dressed in his collar and cuffs, high silk hat and a pair of white kid gloves. Often, Father and Caroline would ride in their carriage for two miles, at which point Father would get out to walk, with the carriage keeping pace with him.[187]

From the collection of the Aurora Historical Society

At the outbreak of the tragic Civil War, Father helped to form the Union Continentals, elder soldiers committed to go to war, if necessary, but more for the purpose of stimulating enlistments in the young men. The *Philadelphia Enquirer* reported he "is a splendid looking man under any circumstances, but let your readers imagine his fine portly figure in handsome

---

[184] Cranston Jones, *Home of the American Presidents*, NY, McGraw-Hill, 1962

[185] Caroline's scrapbook

[186] Snyder

[187] Caroline's scrapbook

Caroline's Roots & Second Marriages

army uniform of blue broadcloth, with sash and sword, epaulettes and continental chapeau and plume, and with the handsome face that he has, he makes altogether the best looking soldier of his age...."[188] He led drill duty for more than a year, performing with his command escort service to military leaving for the field, or the sadder duty of following to their last resting place the honored dust of Buffalo soldiers slain in battle.[189]

On George Washington's birthday in 1862, there was a frightful bonfire in Niagara Square in front of our home. Ten to fifteen cords of wood were saturated with tar; on it burned an effigy of the Confederate president Jefferson Davis. Wild boys were throwing snowballs, and several streetcar windows were broken.[190]

At Lincoln's death in 1865, our house was maliciously smeared with mud, because we showed no signs of mourning; Caroline was sick. Father went out and explained to the gathered crowd that he had not heard of Lincoln's death and then he eulogized Lincoln. Father then headed the citizen's committee to meet the Lincoln funeral train at Batavia on April 26, 1865, to escort it to Buffalo. It was the partisan *Morning Express* that attacked Father so viciously for the lack of mourning. The Republican *Commercial Advertiser* pointed out that no other private homes were draped in mourning. No more patriotic citizen or zealous friend of the Union lives in Buffalo or out of it than Father.[191]

In 1866, we entertained the new President Andrew Johnson. So often, dignitaries included a visit to our home as part of their visit to the grand Niagara Falls. Father liked to point out that the Falls were even a greater curiosity in winter than in summer.[192]

As first citizens of Buffalo, we hosted elite social events, entertaining celebrity visitors, including occasional royal passersby.[193]

---

[188] Caroline's scrapbook

[189] Caroline's scrapbook

[190] Caroline's scrapbook, #15

[191] Rayback, p. 430

[192] MF to George Peabody, Feb. 12, 1867

[193] "The Gate," Forest Lawn, autumn, 1993

Prince Arthur and the Princess of Wales dined with us after visiting Niagara Falls in September of 1860.[194]

As time passed, Father avoided winter travel; he wanted no reliance to be placed on weather and he looked with dread upon the idea of being buried in a snowdrift, more reluctant to take 600-mile trips in the winter than he used to be.[195]

Father installed a kitchen range that burned anthracite coal, a Dutch oven, and a furnace in our home. People walking by delighted in spotting the former president reading in the cozy bay window on the Delaware Avenue side, his favorite sitting place.

From the collection of Aurora Historical Society

Caroline and Father visited Paris, Barcelona, Valencia, Madrid, Malaga and Sevilla in March and April of 1866, in hopes that Caroline's health would improve. Father did report that he disliked the sport of bull-fighting in Spain.[196] They left instructions with me to care for their home; duties included care of the dog Jack, the backyard, barn, carriages and any snow accumulated on the roof and the walks during the winter.[197]

Unlike Father's European tour of 1855, there was little publicity in the papers for this trip. But the *Epoca* in Madrid did write of Father's deep love for art, and that he and his beautiful wife were indefatigable in visiting all the most remarkable museums and galleries.[198]

---

[194] Caroline's scrapbook

[195] Severance, vol. 2, p. 438. MF to I. Harris, Dec. 9, 1868

[196] US Consulate to MF, April 18, 1866

[197] MF to Powers, Dec. 26, 1865. Written as a legal document, signed by CF

[198] Caroline's scrapbook

I wonder if Caroline took her ever-present hammer with her on that trip. She treasured her chipped relics from venerated monuments and buildings, including rare paintings and exquisite Sevres vases that had once belonged to Madame DuBarry, mistress of King Louis XIV of France.[199] Caroline also collected jewelry, diamond rings and pendants, silver, paintings, and furniture. The Paris paper said, "Mrs. Fillmore is one of the leaders of fashion in Paris and displays diamonds with a refreshing brilliancy."[200]

Father showed his great compassion for animals by helping to establish the Buffalo SPCA in 1867, alongside the very capable Miss Lucy Lord. Whenever he witnessed abuse of animals by drovers or drivers, he objected to the intolerable cruelty.

In February of 1868, Father and Caroline were two of the leaders raising funds for the Society of Natural Sciences, hosting a ball at St. James Hall from 8 PM to 2AM.[201]

Father helped to found the auspicious Buffalo Club on Delaware, serving as its first president.

In 1870, Father attended, as he often did, a lecture at the University of Buffalo. It happened to be on the subject of the abuse of alcoholic beverages. The professor asked him if he would like to add some words. He did, saying that he hoped none of the young men present would ever become addicted to the intemperate use of alcohol. Remembering the temptations that surrounded him as a law student, he warned them that as young medical men, many dangers would especially surround them. Even as president of the United States, being required to entertain kings and emperors, he seldom tasted wine or offered it to his guests.

"I have taken but one dose of medicine in thirty years, and that was forced upon me unnecessarily. I attribute my good health to the fact of an originally strong constitution, to an education on a farm, and to life-long habits of regularity and temperance. I never smoked or chewed tobacco. I never knew intoxication. I never allowed my usu-

---

[199] Caroline's scrapbook

[200] Caroline's scrapbook

[201] Caroline's scrapbook

al hours for sleep to be interrupted. The Sabbath I always kept as a day of rest. Besides being a religious duty, it was essential to health."[202]

On his 70th birthday, Father said, "God's finger touched me, and I simply did my best."

Father gathered his four remaining Fillmore siblings in Scio, Michigan, for a summer family reunion in 1873: Olive Johnson--75, Father--73, Cyrus--71, Calvin--63 and Julia Harris from California--61. Both of my aunts were widows. The five Fillmores posed for a proud picture, in order of ages. A friend described Father's appearance; his "hair is whiter and a little thinner, but he has the same erect and full rounded form, smooth skin with scarcely a wrinkle. He said he had not varied in weight more than ten pounds since he was President."[203]

From the collection of the Aurora Historical Society

In the late sixties, I visited Saratoga with my stepmother. Unfortunately, we had to eat breakfast in the dark by gaslight. I want to point out that her temper was never controlled even by Father; she never deferred even to him. But I knew she was endlessly proud of Father. She commissioned portraits and busts that were all over our home, and she donated to organizations which Father had begun and valued.[204]

In Father's will, he recognized the tension between his wife and me: "I feel it a duty and a pleasure to record my dying testimony to the noble qualities of my beloved wife Caroline, who has ever proved a kind, affectionate and devoted wife, and…if she and my son Millard Powers shall

---

[202] Severance, Vol. X, 1907

[203] Caroline's scrapbook

[204] "The Gate," Forest Lawn, autumn 1993

both survive me, I hope and trust that they may love each other as I have loved them; and as they will both be orphans, indeed, I hope also that they will mutually render to each other every assistance due from a most affectionate parent to a beloved child, and from a most affectionate and dutiful child to a beloved parent; and with this I shall rest in peace."

Chapter Eleven

CAROLINE'S TROUBLED WIDOWHOOD

Father's sudden death on March 8 of 1874 only made Caroline more infirm, nervous, eccentric and temperamental. The Buffalo paper wrote, "Buffalo mourns the loss of her greatest, worthiest and best citizen."[205] Caroline began a fierce seclusion, a great change taking over her character; the imperious and refined lady gradually metamorphosed into a chronic lunatic, with capricious outbursts of profanity and rage. Delusions and hallucinations became her reality.[206] I eventually moved uptown to the third floor of a downtown business building (incidentally my dear friend, Grover Cleveland, also lived there), leaving Caroline alone with only her servants.[207]

In 1877, Caroline paid a visit to Clifton Springs where Dr. Foster noticed that she was much changed from previous visits, being very excitable and moody. He suspected that she may be using liquor and morphine. One of her servants reported that when she was visited by some revivalists, she shouted, "Hell is let loose, and the hounds are after me!"[208] Her profanity ran amok—"My God…devilish…damn such people…curse the name of Fillmore," and more that was not her accustomed manner of speech. She complained to her dressmaker, Susan Campbell, that "those cussed ladies came here and talked me to death. Cuss them, I wish I had some infernal

---

[205] *Buffalo Press*, March 10, 1874

[206] *The Fillmore Will Case*, Dr. Landon Gray

[207] *Children in the White House*, p. 140

[208] Gray

screwdriver to screw up their everlasting tongue...."[209]

In January of 1879, she first began her new hobby of writing her will. She created a fifty-page handwritten will with Orasmus Marshall, her legal adviser since Father's death. In it she left bequests to institutions, relatives and friends totaling nearly $100,000 [in 2024 dollars, $2,800,000]. She gave a Rubens and a Hudson River School painting by James Hart to the Buffalo Fine Arts Academy. Father's and Caroline's thousand-volume library would go to the Buffalo Historical Society.[210] The Washington Street Baptist Church received $4000, partly from the sale of her pew. The University of Rochester received $20,000 [in 2024 dollars, $560,000], one fourth "as a memorial fund in honor of Millard Fillmore by his affectionate widow; another fourth in honor of the late Ezekiel McIntosh, my first husband, by his affectionate widow; another fourth in honor of my father, the late Charles Carmichael; the last fourth in honor of the late Dr. Absalom Blachley, who was himself deeply interested in the cause of education--my mother's brother."[211]

Also remembered was the Buffalo Orphan Asylum, $4000; Buffalo General Hospital, $4000; the YMCA, $2000; the Buffalo Historical Society, $2000; Buffalo Home of the Friendless, $1000; Buffalo Society of Natural Sciences, $1000; and the SPCA, $500. The Buffalo Fine Arts Academy received $2000 plus ancient antiques, miniatures, jewelry, paintings, chromos, lithographs, engravings, and Roman mosaics. May I point out that Father helped to found the hospital, the YMCA, the historical society, the science museum, the SPCA and the Fine Arts Academy.

She remembered her friend Miss Sophia Condit of Utica with her "diamond cluster finger ring of seven diamonds, a point lace handkerchief and antique collar (not her finest), and some Honiton lace." For Miss Julia Condit, she left her brown lava set, a brooch and pendant earrings of Bacchus and grapes, a set of buttons, also a handkerchief and antique collar (not her

---

[209] Spencer Clinton's trial summary, 1884

[210] "The Gate," Forest Lawn, autumn 1993

[211] Caroline's first will, January 15, 1879

Caroline's Troubled Widowhood

Caroline's dress
Courtesy of The Buffalo History Museum

finest), two pairs of sleeves, and a yard and a half of lace.[212] Mrs. Solomon Haven, the widow of Father's partner, received fancy furniture, a landscape painted by Caroline, many diamonds, several India cashmere square shawls, and a blue-black silk velvet dress made and embroidered in Paris. The Havens daughters, Miss Netty and Miss Ida, both received rings with nine and ten diamonds, respectively, more jewelry, and additional elegant accessories. Mrs. Millicent Marshall received a painting by Caroline, "Lakes of Killarney, Ireland." All in all, Caroline gave away six rings with multiple diamonds in each.[213]

To Miss Lucy Lord, founder of the local SPCA, Caroline gave "a brooch with the head of Pio Nono on a black stone, said to resemble Mr. Fillmore, cut in Rome in 1855."[214]

She left me furniture and jewelry that had belonged to Mother and to Abby, family portraits, and Father's papers.[215] I received a picture of a boy with a feather in his cap that was presented to Abby by the artist named King. Caroline returned to me a music box and two small plaster casts that I had gifted to her. Abby's rosewood piano, the harp and their stools, as well as her music books, were treasures to me. The oak high back chair that Mother had embroidered, the harp music stand, and Abby's guitar natu-

---

[212] Ibid

[213] Ibid

[214] Ibid

[215] "The Gate," Forest Lawn, autumn 1993

rally came to me as well. She also left me Father's correspondence and law library, as well as the personal ornaments belonging to Mother and my sister.

The servants were properly acknowledged in this first will. John Jamieson, her coachman, received her large carriage, coupe, and the span of horses, so that he could make a living after her death, as well as $1000, so that he could pay off the mortgage held by Father on his house and lot. Jamieson's twin children, named Millard Fillmore Jamieson and Caroline Fillmore Jamieson, each received $500 and a hope that "they will live to be a blessing to their parents and an honor to their names."[216] And the servants were carefully remembered to receive Caroline's underwear.

But as she aged, she became vindictive and litigious; her speech became thick and indistinct. In the summer of 1879, she called out to Jamieson, who was in the library with her, "Come here, John! See there, John, don't you see the devil there watching me?"

"No ma'am, there is none there."

"There is, John, there is."

Three times she came into her seamstress, wearing a mask showing a young girl with blue eyes and flaxen hair. She claimed she had a drawer full of them and that she used to go to the theatre with her distinguished husband wearing them.[217]

Servant Nellie Kelly, Caroline's servant in '78 and '79, reported her mistress's anger at pillowcases that did not fit the pillows was such that she literally foamed at the mouth, stamped around the room, and shook her fist at her. "You would love to get a knife and cut my throat, if you dared." Another time, Caroline noticed a broken dish on the dining room table, took another dish and pounded the broken one with it until the latter was in small pieces, cutting the tablecloth in many places.[218]

The cook reported that when Caroline was unhappy with her beef tea, she insisted that the cook taste it. When she refused, Caroline poured half

---

[216] Caroline's first will

[217] Spencer Clinton's trial summary, 1884

[218] Ibid

the tea over the cook and pushed her violently against the cupboard. "I am the boss in my own house," she declared. The stories from the servants go on and on—slamming doors, talking to herself, throwing keys, screaming, lashing everything with a whip. She made threats and accusations—she told one maid that the staff would find her some morning with a rope around her neck. That maid left our service because she was afraid of being killed. When another maid was bathing her, Caroline accused the girl of trying to drown her.[219]

Dora Kessler reported that one Sunday when Caroline was going to church, she said, "When I ring the bell, you come upstairs." When Dora came upstairs, Caroline had the wardrobe upside down and emptied. She said, "There's some of my things gone. I don't say you took them, but it was someone. It may be years and years ago. I have not been to the wardrobe since a year." Dora tried to help her dress, but Caroline, pacing and shaking her fist at her, said, "Go 'way, you are just as bad as all the rest of them. You act like the devil himself…Not for love or money can I get anyone to do anything for me. My God, my God, will I never get rest? No, never, till I take a razor and cut my throat, then they will all come and dance on my grave and say, 'Here lies poor Mrs. Fillmore.'"[220]

Another day, Dora was trying to help Caroline into her gloves, but she kept wiggling her fingers so incessantly, it could not be done. Finally, after a half hour of struggle, Caroline said angrily, "Why don't you put on my glove?!"

"I can't, because you don't keep still," Dora retorted angrily.

"How dare you speak to me like that!" responded Caroline.[221]

Another time she informed John that the devil was chasing her through the room and pinching her. When she became angry with her paid companion, Annie Ryan, Caroline accused her of wanting to kill her mistress, insisting that Jamieson should go to the police station for an officer. Caro-

---

[219] Ibid

[220] Ibid

[221] Ibid

line had forgotten that she had an electric telegraph alarm in the house by which she could summon an officer.[222]

In the spring of 1880, Jamieson drove Caroline to church in the sleigh in two fresh inches of snow. But after church the snow was gone. Jamieson took her friend Mrs. Gordon and Caroline to the Gordon's Morgan Street home, dragging the coupe over bare stones. When he tried to take her straight home, she argued, "I want my usual drive."[223]

So John drove her up Morgan Street very slowly, then onto Palmer and West (a wooden pavement that didn't pull as hard) and out to William Fargo's home on Niagara. Suddenly, she became greatly excited, yelling and screaming, punching him in the back with her little rattan cane. "Why don't you drive me somewhere else and not run me over the rocks and stones? Do you want to kill me?"[224]

She insisted on being taken over to Prospect Avenue, then another avenue.[225]

When they got home, the horses were all foaming and heated from dragging the sleigh over stones. She said to him, "I will fix you for this. You tried to kill me, but you couldn't."[226]

Caroline complained that she had sacrificed her life for seventeen long years for the name of Fillmore. "Curse the name of Fillmore," she'd shout, occasionally accusing him of having cheated and wronged her.

Early one morning, she went out to the stable, told the coachman that the servants would give her nothing to eat and insisted he drive her to the hospital at Virginia and Delaware for breakfast.

In September, Caroline called an attorney named Sizer, wanting to draft a new will. She did not want Sizer to come to her home, claiming that her original lawyer, Orasmus Marshall, had all her servants in his pay, spying on her. She did not want Marshall to know about these changes, so she

---

[222] Gray
[223] Clinton
[224] Gray
[225] Clinton
[226] Clinton

insisted on not laying eyes on the new attorney, or meeting in his office or her own home. But even in her friend's home, Caroline would not meet with Sizer, insisting that she would pass notes to him from upstairs—very confusing notes that necessitated many trips between the two for four days. She made Sizer go out the back way, so that he would not be seen by anyone. She was especially fearful that her coachman, John Jamieson, who had served Caroline for sixteen years. would hear that his employer, the widow of a president, was bold enough to make a will without his knowledge.[227]

She disinherited her servants and several friends, and reduced or cancelled her bequests to several Buffalo organizations. The whole Jamieson family was removed from her will, as well as servants Bridget Conroy and Ann Ryan. Caroline claimed that Jamieson had become intemperate, careless, drunk, and negligent, and that he had endangered her life in driving, and that her patience was exhausted.[228]

She took back $10,000 she'd promised to the historical society, as well as $10,000 to the Fine Arts Academy. But she did add a gift of bed linen to the hospital and a marble bust of Father given to the YMCA.[229]

The codicil carefully parsed out singular pieces of silver—a ladle to Miss Gorham, a fish knife to Mrs. Whitcomb. Mrs.

Cardboard Millard visits his burial site at Forest Lawn—Photo by Sarah Jagodzinski

---

[227] Gray

[228] Clinton

[229] Caroline's codicil, May 8, 1880

J. V. Beam received "one maccaroni shovel." In all, 99 pieces of silver were individually assigned to thirty different people. Marshall was fired as executor of her estate, appointing George Gorham in his place.[230]

Finally, she had to meet face to face with Sizer to have the will read to her and attested. During the reading, she was flippant, girlish, paying more attention to her dress and hair than to her will.

In June of 1880, Caroline traveled to Gettysburg with a party of friends, but she made things uncomfortable by declaring her dislike of one of the ladies. Mrs. Jewett reported that the head waiter at the hotel expressed his hope that everything had been satisfactory. Caroline had violently scolded him that "she had been all over the world and had never been in a place before where she could get nothing to eat." Mrs. Jewett left the table in embarrassment.[231]

Caroline claimed she had not a relative in the world, although she had five first cousins, and obviously, me.

In October of 1880, Caroline suffered a stroke of paralysis due to cerebral hemorrhage. She never regained the use of her right paralyzed side. She lost her speech; all she could say was, "I say…I say the truth…yes and no." Occasionally she managed to scream wildly for five minutes every morning and every evening, as one might take a cocktail before dinner.

Her second and final stroke came on August 11 of 1881 at the age of 67.

As a result, in 1881 I and others brought suit against her estate. She had not been herself. And much of the contested property was Father's before he ever married Caroline. I was particularly interested in the silver set that Father had ordered for my mother on leaving the White House. Caroline claimed it had been presented to her first husband. Caroline was memorialized in St. Paul's Cathedral, then buried in Forest Lawn with Millard, Abigail, and Abby.

One of my attorneys was my friend Grover Cleveland, and we did succeed. The mansion was inexplicably left to George Gorham, the executor

---

[230] Gray

[231] Gray

of her will. The case was finally resolved in my favor in the NYS Court of Appeals.

I was the lone surviving member of the formerly happy Fillmore family.

Chapter Twelve

POSTSCRIPT AND AUTHOR'S NOTES

After Caroline's death, Powers spent his evenings in the lobby of the Tifft Hotel at 477 Main Street, his last residence, talking or playing cards with his friends. He died at age 61 at the hotel on November 15 of 1889, a mere year after his resolution of the appeal against Caroline's wills. "Lacking the necessity to labor, and having no one dependent upon him for support, he was deprived of two strong incentives to active and aggressive work in his chosen profession."[232]

He left substantial gifts to the SPCA and to the Society for the Prevention of Cruelty to Children.[233]

In his later years, he often expressed that no man should start in life alone, that he should marry, and have a home and friends and the comforts which a family and children are sure to bring.[234]

The twelve-piece set of silver plates made in 1853 from the proceeds of the sale of the fancy carriage was a central issue in the court case against Caroline Fillmore. Its whereabouts are still unknown.

The massive Fillmore mansion became the Castle Inn. "Though again refitted, and converted into a fashionable hotel, the original style of the house has been carefully preserved. The drawing room is just as it used to be. Here are the curious-shaped mirrors that tell no tales, although they have reflected many a company of distinguished guests; also, the heavy

---

[232] MPF obituary

[233] Memorial Meeting of the Erie County Bar Asso., 1890

[234] Ibid

cornices, quaint cabinets, odd-shaped pieces of rosewood furniture, and French tapestry rug. In a niche on the main stairway a marble bust of President Fillmore looks out upon the new-old scene. To the taste and generous investment of a woman, Buffalo owes the careful restoration and preservation of a historical house...."[235]

Frances Folsom Cleveland's mother, Emma Harmon Folsom Perrine, stayed at the Castle Inn as a bride in 1889, after she had stayed several seasons in the White House.

By 1929, the Castle Inn was razed to make room for the present Statler Hotel, overlooking the McKinley Monument and the majestic Art Deco masterpiece, Buffalo City Hall. A plaque remembering Fillmore's home is on the west side of the hotel at street level.

In front of Buffalo City Hall on the southwest side, overlooking his former home and the city he loved and served, is a statue of Millard Fillmore. It was created by Bryant Baker, erected by the State of New York, and unveiled in 1932. Inscribed at the base is "Lawyer, Educator, Philanthropist, Statesman."

The Buffalo Fine Arts Academy evolved into the world-renowned AKG (Albright Knox Gudren Art Gallery.)

The Buffalo Historical Society is now the Buffalo History Museum.

The Buffalo Society of Natural Sciences is now the Buffalo Museum of Science.

The University of Buffalo is now part of the statewide SUNY system.

Abby's harp and square rosewood piano that graced the White House library are now in East Aurora's Millard Fillmore Presidential Site. Also displayed there are the bound volumes of Abby's music, showcasing the Fillmores' cultural taste. The harp and music stand, gifted to Abby by her beau, Hiram Day, are also at the Millard Fillmore Presidential Site.

The White House Library now has three shelves just for Bibles alone in 75 languages for foreign visitors to use.

Millard's sister Julia Harris from California was the grandmother of

---

[235] "The Odgen Family in America" genealogy, 1907, p. 216

Charlie Chaplin's 16-year-old first wife, Mildred Harris. She had been a child actress from the age of 10, born in 1901, and married to Chaplin from 1918 to 1920.

About all those stories and encyclopedia entries about the Fillmores putting in the first White House bathtub--H.L. Mencken started all that. In 1917, to add a bit of humor to the dire news of the Great World War, he concocted a fictional history of the bathtub, "A Neglected Anniversary." In it, he used manufactured citations and bogus statistics, assigning Fillmore as the first president to install a White House bathtub. Eight years later, in "Melancholy Reflections," he mocked the gullibility of the American public and retracted his invented "facts," in vain. In 1949 he wrote, "the success of this idle hoax, done in time of war, when more serious writing was impossible, vastly astonished me. It was taken gravely by a great many other newspapers, and presently made its way into medical literature and into standard reference books. It had, of course, no truth in it whatsoever, and I more than once confessed publicly that it was only a jocosity... Scarcely a month goes by that I do not find the substance of it reprinted, not as foolishness but as fact, and not only in newspapers but in official documents and other works of highest pretensions."[236]

Thurlow Weed, who was at first Fillmore's political sponsor, became his worst enemy. After Fillmore's death, Weed used his powerful Albany voice to write a scathing review of his former friend in Weed's own autobiography.[237]

Fillmore Glen is a state park in Moravia that hosts a replica of the Fillmore log cabin in which Millard was born. A stream-fed swimming pool, waterfalls, and hiking trails make it a worthy stop. Not far away are the

---

[236] Mencken, H.L., *A Mencken Chrestomathy*

[237] Rayback, p. 443

sites of Fillmore's birth and his boyhood home. See https://parks.ny.gov/parks/fillmoreglen/ for more information.

The Millard Fillmore Presidential Site is the only remaining home of the Fillmores, other than the White House. It is also the only presidential home built by the president himself.[238] Run by volunteers, all tours from April 1 through October 31 are by reservation only at least 48 hours or more in advance by calling 716-652-2621. The Aurora Historical Society acquired the house in 1975, restoring it to circa 1826. The house now typifies a small frame dwelling of the Federal Period. The house is furnished with many pieces that belonged to the Fillmores from their East Aurora, White House, and Buffalo years. https://www.aurorahistoricalsociety.com/pages/millard-fillmore-presidential-site

---

[238] The only exception is the Hardscrabble log cabin built by Grant in Missouri and only occupied by his family and unhappy wife for three months.

Postscript and Author's Notes

AUTHOR'S NOTE: My own path to this Fillmore obsession began in my childhood when my Second Baptist Church of Auburn, NY, held its annual Sunday School picnics at the Fillmore Glen. Then, on moving to East Aurora as a young mom, my mother-in-law involved me as a docent in the newly opened Millard Fillmore Museum. She also challenged me to write Fillmore's Lincolnesque story. I've since written *Will the Real Millard Fillmore Please Stand Up?,* appeared on C-SPAN's *Presidential Portrait* series, written a song on his life, and made costumed appearances and lectures as Abigail. My Eggert Elementary School Young Yorkers History Club published a book, *Secrets Along the Niagara: the Underground Railroad in Western New York*, following a thorough study of local town historians' reports on UGRR activity and many local field trips to UGRR sites.

Since retiring, I have visited presidential sites in chronological order. I am currently up to #23, Benjamin Harrison. Before each visit, I read a biography or two on the upcoming president. This has turned out to be a highly effective American history learning project, as the issues and side characters in all of the presidential stories are interconnected and illuminating.

As a young mom beginning my research on Millard Fillmore, I read with judgment Caroline's detailed will. Now with more life experience, I see that she may have suffered from Alzheimer's or dementia, thus explaining her bizarre behavior. Our knowledge on this debilitating disease continues to grow.

History is made up of people's stories--their failings and motivations and triumphs. I do believe decision-makers' intentions need to be examined in the context of their times, avoiding an excessive "presentism." However, I find many parallels and connections to the times in which we live. As George Santayana said, "Those who don't know history are doomed to repeat it."

www.ingramcontent.com/pod-product-compliance
Lightning Source LLC
Chambersburg PA
CBHW072201100426
42738CB00011BA/2498